I0041001

Global Women in the Start-up World

Global Women in the Start-up World

Conversations in Silicon Valley

Marta Zucker

BEP BUSINESS EXPERT PRESS

Global Women in the Start-up World: Conversations in Silicon Valley

Copyright © Business Expert Press, LLC, 2018.

All rights reserved. No part of this publication may be reproduced, stored in a retrieval system, or transmitted in any form or by any means—electronic, mechanical, photocopy, recording, or any other except for brief quotations, not to exceed 400 words, without the prior permission of the publisher.

First published in 2018 by
Business Expert Press, LLC
222 East 46th Street, New York, NY 10017
www.businessexpertpress.com

ISBN-13: 978-1-94744-169-9 (paperback)
ISBN-13: 978-1-94744-170-5 (e-book)

Business Expert Press Entrepreneurship and Small Business Management Collection

Collection ISSN: 1946-5653 (print)
Collection ISSN: 1946-5661 (electronic)

Cover and interior design by Exeter Premedia Services Private Ltd., Chennai, India

First edition: 2018

10 9 8 7 6 5 4 3 2 1

Printed in the United States of America.

Abstract

My newest book "**Global Women in the Start-up World: Conversations in Silicon Valley**" (May 2016) (Polish title "Kobiety globalne w świecie start-upów. Rozmowy w Dolinie Krzemowej) is a selection of interview-driven stories told by the Polish female founders who successfully made it to Silicon Valley. The introductions to the book are by Ari Horie, Founder and CEO of Women's Startup Lab, and by Professor Piotr Moncarz of Stanford University.

The interviewees: Patrycja Slawuta "SelfHackathon"; Ela Madej "50 Years"; Julia Krysztofiak-Szopa, Amelia Krysztofiak "Wellfitting"; Kate Scisel "Contact IQ"; Zuzanna Stańska "DailyArt, Moiseum"; Kamila Sidor "Geek Girls Carrots."

I decided to write a book with the focus on female founders because although women are playing an increasingly important role in the technology and business worlds, they still face unique challenges and hurdles which can be particularly acute in the fast-paced start-up environment.

My interviewees came from Poland to Silicon Valley and succeeded, they never gave up. Today they became role models for many young women. They ignored the glass ceiling. They built their networks; they dealt with sexism. They followed their dreams, mastered the art of running a global company. Silicon Valley can be intimidating but with my book as a guide one can navigate the most challenging aspects of being a woman in the start-up world. What many learned from these stories is that you don't have to give up your femininity to fit into a male-dominated industry; you can be yourself and make a difference. The stories in the book also prove that foreign start-up founders are welcome in Silicon Valley and that they can achieve truly global success. It doesn't matter what country you are from—you can build your start-up in any country: some of my interviewees live and work in Poland, while others decided to move abroad.

The book is a follow-up to last year's publication: "Talent Olympics in Silicon Valley: Conversations with Start-up Masters" (September 2015) (Polish title: "Igrzyska talentów w Dolinie Krzemowej. Rozmowy z mistrzami start-upów").

Both books have been very well received in the start-up, business, and academic communities and within days both publications became best-selling books. The books were published in Poland by PWN, the leading Polish provider of scientific, educational, and professional literature.

Keywords

diversity, female founder, glass ceiling, interview, millennials, silicon valley, start-up, technology

Contents

Acknowledgments

Translated by Anna Samborska and Clay Young.

Introduction

Piotr Moncarz is a Consulting Professor of Civil and the Department of Environmental Engineering at Stanford University. He is the founder and Chairman of the Polish-American Trade Council. He also works as Principal Engineer for Exponent Inc. in Menlo Park, California.

The talent contests[1] are not just a part of the culture of innovation but also a part of the social reality in which women—unlike in the earlier days of the industrial revolution, where the key developments where introduced by men—are becoming integral to the innovation revolution. In this world creativity and technical know-how are combined sparking new, necessary, and desirable solutions. This is a key phenomenon.

Traditionally, Polish women of middle and upper classes received good education, although it rarely included science and technology, with celebrated Maria Skłodowska-Curie being a notable exception. The situation changed radically during the Polish People's Republic (PRL) where the post-war rebuilding of the country and later the necessity of second income in households "invited" women to applied sciences and engineering colleges.

During PRL it was declared that a woman could do any physical labor just like a man. Of course it was a complete misconception, since regardless of physical ability, this was not where the intellectual strength of women lay. Women learned how to be foremen in construction, how to drive a tractor, but the whole process was a way of forcing women to turn into men. There were fields where women found their niches— in medicine, biology, and laboratory work. There women could create their own world. Teaching at schools was taken over by women—partly because of their skills, partly because jobs in education were so badly paid

---

[1] Referral to Marta Zucker's book: "Talent Olympics in Silicon Valley: Conversations with Start-up Masters" Warsaw 2015.

that a man working there could not support a family and women could not find other jobs worthy of their education and talents.

The idea of turning a woman into a man was bad but broke certain barriers. For a while now I've been following Girls Go Start-up! program in Poland. It is the first academy for start-up women. Do we really need it? I am not sure. But perhaps it is easier for women to create start-ups when they are in the company of other women who also try to create something rather than in an environment full of ambitious male entrepreneurs. Maybe there will be a new system in which companies would be divided into male- and female-run. Yet if we do not change the traditional view of start-ups, which assumes that they are founded by young ambitious males, we will lose the opportunity to create new and important innovations, which in that case might never appear on the market.

Innovation, as practiced in Silicon Valley, involves creating something original, even groundbreaking, something that would respond to the needs of both the entrepreneur and the consumer, something that involves great empathy. In empathy women are much better than men. Women listen better than men, are better tuned into emotions, which are very important in creating new solutions. There are still certain blocks in this area, as for instance the fact that women, even in leadership positions in start-ups, still tend to hide behind their male colleagues' backs. Also when they talk about their passions they do it in a much more subdued way than a male would. I think it stems from the fear of misjudgment, of being labeled as "pushy."

In serious innovative endeavors we see more and more women in senior positions. It doesn't surprise me. It surprises me that it took so long. Is this a process that will develop naturally, organically or will it require special nurturing and attention? Today it is too early to tell.

In the modern world there are very many educated women who do not wish to be an extra labor. They want to be leaders in the full sense of the word, so also in the areas where creative thinking is taking place, where innovations are born. This is a very important phenomenon. The Western world has already integrated women into professional life. Still, it is still common in some countries that a woman gets paid less than a man for the same work. There are many places where changes need to take place but the general tendency of integration is now irreversible.

In "Top 500 Innovators," a very successful program for young scientists and people involved in the transfer of technology at Polish universities, women made up one-third of the participants and in some groups even 50 percent. Initially men were indeed more active but this trend evens out very quickly, or even changes altogether. Women in "Top 500 Innovators" did very well. Not only did they actively organize team-work in workshops, where the object was to solve actual problems but also played an important role in everyday group integration. The program was nine weeks long. It is a long time for people who had not known each other before and during the program lived and worked 24/7. It was the women who led the way in organizing event and suggesting new ideas.

The role of women among the program graduates is significant. A woman chairs the Top 500 Association and there are many women on the board. When I follow their news from Poland I hear the voices of women more often than those of men. It means that some energy got released that is just as creative as the traditional male one, but maybe even stronger.

Female bosses are often called "strong, hardcore women" when they are tough and ruthless. Yet when a man fires or reprimands someone this is considered normal managerial behavior. This is because women are expected not to be tough but soft, "motherly." It is something worth thinking about.

It's been said that Silicon Valley is like great Olympics where you go after 1,000 hours of training and previous setbacks. A woman needs to be just as well prepared as a man. Competence cannot be substituted by personal charm. At some point in her life a woman enters her societal-biological role—a fundamental, natural role in human life. And I think this plays a role in those Olympic games. When a team applies for funding as one of many, each having their own pitch, team presentation, the risk of losing a leader mid-way occurs to the decision makers, who are usually men. It is understandable. It is important to convince them that I am doing well and my approach to career and personal life is realistic and responsible.

Susan Wojcicki, a de facto co-founder of Google and today a CEO of YouTube, said once that it was possible to have a family and kids and a career. Still, one must remember that they are not parallel matters but are integrated and there's no point pretending to the world that it's otherwise. Susan Wojcicki speaks plainly about it. And I think such straightforward approach is the better one. To me it is so convincing that I would imme-diately bet on the team with such a woman rather than on an all-male one. Women need to learn such plain talk and understand that they lose a lot trying to convince people they were as good as men. They have to focus on the fact that they are great human beings who can create "some-thing" even in a situation when they are raising children and are leading a big company. This approach might help women to be less aggressive in their career and their fight for it. If you are feeling persecuted just because you are a woman, of because you are "different" it brings out aggression which not just prevents you from winning but even puts people off. These are the matters that young potential start-uppers should learn.

In Silicon Valley, in Poland, and in many other places in the world, today and a 100 years ago there are many examples of women acting just as well or even better than men. Yet we must stress that today's progress lies in teamwork. Today no one questions women's essential competence. The 19th century nonsense has been retired. However, there is still little experience of work in integrated male-female teams so we should focus on how to make this process more efficient. While dealing with a mixed female–male team where a traditional male feeling of "high worth" is likely to arise, men cooperating with women must show culture, acquired at home or at school and if that's not enough there should be external legal regulations and internal code of conduct which will not tolerate deviation in this area.

—*Piotr Moncarz*
Consulting Professor, Stanford University

Open Letter

Ari Horie, founder and CEO of Women's Startup Lab—an accelerator in Silicon Valley supporting start-ups founded by women. Ari comes from Japan. She is the winner of many prestigious awards and rankings, including Women of Influence in Silicon Valley 2015 according to "Silicon Valley Business Journal," 10 Visionary Women of 2014 of CNN and The 40 Women To Watch Over 40 2015.

Desire

When you want to start something, you need to ask yourself whether it is a good idea: Are you really passionate about it? Do you really want to do it? People often have a desire to do something, but there is always a part of you that says, "I don't want to do it because I might fail." If it goes well, it is exciting... the "yes" part is there, but the "no" part shows up when we begin to fail. Entrepreneurs are usually optimistic: they are so excited and so committed to the changes they will facilitate that their inner passion and their desire drive them to become successful. The other part, though, is solely business, can you create value that others will pay for? If your business is not making money, then it's actually a great hobby. So you can be a great hobby person; the question is, can you generate revenue from your hobby or from your passions? We often get so excited about what we want to do that we forget about what customers really want and that leads to an unsuccessful business.

Women have a very small number of role models. Women lack a business culture, the culture that it's OK to talk about our business. Most of the time we talk about our other personal things to establish connections! We talk about *saving* money but not about *making* money. And those are two very different ways of thinking and approaching the world. Women have smaller circles of business resources and networks to help with their business. So it is challenging, but the challenge doesn't mean that it's impossible. As a female entrepreneur knowing the background and landscape of our business environment, I would say, make sure that you are willing to go through the hardship and don't give up, don't listen to those who suggest that you can't do it, because there is always a chance of winning and you just have to bet on that chance. Believe in the 2 percent, even though 98 percent fail. Think differently and have a unique strategy to be that 2 percent winner.

"Just Do It"

Entrepreneurship is also about personality. When I was 10 years old I saw a documentary on TV about the Japanese Department at Warsaw University. The students were so bright: they knew more about Japanese history than an average Japanese, and their language skills were much better than most Japanese people. I was so impressed!

I thought it would be great if one of those students became my "pen pal." So I wrote a letter. But where to send it? On the envelope I wrote only: "To any student learning Japanese at Warsaw University, Warsaw, Poland." I was so excited about the possibility of having a friend at Warsaw University that I didn't really care that it might not arrive. I didn't really care if sending a letter without an address wouldn't work… I just did it. The possibility was far too exciting for me as a 10-year-old girl, I couldn't not act. I got reply from Maggy; she came to visit me in Hiroshima. Today, my Polish "pen pal" lives in Japan and after 35 years, we are still friends! Let your passion lead you, not your fear of failure!

I think entrepreneurship is being so excited about something that is so important to you. So passionate that you cannot help but take action, and no matter what happens you keep going. You must be truly faithful to your passion and finding your voice … And let it sing!

Have a Strategy

Silicon Valley right now is not known for its openness; it has also gotten a bit of a male model. If you want to come to Silicon Valley as a start-up founder and a woman, don't just show up. When coming to Silicon Valley you need a strategy; just as when you start a business, you need a strategy. Try to go through an accelerator where you can anchor yourself with other female entrepreneurs, local influencers are a must. Silicon Valley is open and friendly but people often mistake that as "easy." It gives that impression but this is the center where the global best of the best gather. There is no second chance if you present yourself poorly at VCs (Venture Capitalists). Why should there be? They have hundreds of start-ups knocking on their doors. You need to start building your network immediately. Also find out what kind of investors are here. And last but not least, assess, find out for yourself what is really important in your life and make sure your strategies for your life and for your start-up are aligned. Don't get mad at VCs when they expect you to give up everything else for success... Don't get in bed with them before you clearly understand what they want and their expectations for you.

In my opinion, what is really different between women and men, is that women are often fulfilled by different things in life. Women often value and get fulfillment from relationships, community, and people. Even if they have a career and even if they are successful, they still feel that the "human" part is important. So know what fulfills you and be sure that your start-up journey is part of the puzzle... or end up one of those super successful people that are so unfulfilled, unhappy with their personal life falling apart. Make sure to ask what success you want in your *life*, not just in your career or business.

To create this ultimate success at WSLab (Women's Startup Lab) we revisit and redefine success as whole: we make sure you have considered this other part of your life too; we make sure that you would be fulfilled, optimized, aligned to function at your best. This way you ultimately become the most powerful and the start-up CEO most likely to succeed. Because you might have a business that is going to make millions of dollars. That's great, but meantime create around your life a structure that will allow you to actually have what matters to you. I highly recommend that as a woman with a start-up, you build your life *designed* such that you run your start-up and your start-up doesn't run you.

24/7

Is it possible to run a successful start-up and have a family? You have to define what success means to you. If you are trying to have a typical

Silicon Valley success, which is raising millions of dollars and growing really fast, then you have to think about it. There are people that are devoting every single minute of every single hour to achieving that success. Are you going to be like that? Or do you have enough money to employ somebody to grow your company? God gave us 24 hours a day—everybody has 24 hours and some might have a more powerful network, team, brain, or money, than others but at the end of the day we all have limitations. What's great about this is that you just have to put the puzzle pieces together by assessing what you can accomplish *within* the limitations. The problem is everyone thinks trying harder and asking for more money will get you success. No! Accept the limitations on time and money then be creative in getting things done with extreme measures if you want extraordinary success in life.

I actually *don't* think you can have it all. You can say that you can have it all but it has to be your individual definition of what's in it and how much. Some people think that the definition of being a good mom is being really patient with your kids, cooking healthy meals, managing playdates and social lives, spending a lot time with them, throwing big birthday parties, and having kids that are playing sports, are well balanced, smart, playing music, piano, all that stuff.

And having a husband who is really committed and having a great relationship with all of them.

But remember that if changing the world—having a start-up that makes an impact in the world—matters to you, for the next few years you may need to redefine "being a mom" differently. You need to redefine the standard, not follow the standard, you need to be a confident parent to communicate your mission in life, keep strong values in your in family regardless of crazy hours. Do not waste your time saying "sorry" to your kids or feeling guilty. Just like your employees need you to lead them with confidence in any challenging time, a parent needs to lead their kids with confidence in keeping the family values intact. So you *can* have it all as long as you design your life around the 24-hour limit. That's really clear; it is that simple, actually. But doing it requires discipline, focus, strategy, and design—just like a business. You just have to find the right answer for yourself.

Accept your priorities, own them, design around them, get help instead of feeling sorry or guilty and overwhelmed with everything on your plate. Yes, we women have more work to do, it's not easy, but we are doing it, and we are successful. Your start-up is like your other baby: it requires commitment and adjustments from everything in your life for it to grow.

Can you have a "life-style" start-up and be wildly successful? If you can only have five hours per day for your start-up, it can be successful but it might take 15 years. If you want to do it in five years, you need to give a lot of hours. If you want to work five hours a day, and you want to grow your company in five years, then you probably have to invest money. So now money is compensating for your freedom. People will look at you and say it's a compromise, you are not spending as much time with your kids. But that's not a compromise… the message is: You chose it. It is a perfect balance for you.

In Women's Startup Lab we look at how we can redefine your success clearly, and how we can surround you with powerful resources and advisors to accelerate your success.

What I Wish I Knew

I wish somebody told me 15 years ago that as a young person you actually have so much already! You don't *need* to be wiser, you don't need to live in a "someday when I have…" future. Be open to learning and gaining more experience but also be deeply aware of the power of youth and vitality, the freedom to think and act that often diminishes as we get older. I wish somebody told me to be present with who I was in my wonderful twenties, asked me to focus equally on what I already had and on staying humble and learning. I always thought that I was not good enough yet as young person. I would remind others they are powerful now and embrace living life in the now: You are already so awesome, and you are perfect.

Letting young people know that they already have something that other people don't have and giving them the power to appreciate themselves and to design their career and personal life based on what they already have is very important. So, challenge everything you know! The earlier you discover that you can break the code, break the rules, to create something new, the faster you find the path to your success, and the better insight you gain about your own gifts and talents.

What I really wish is that when I was 20 years old someone had simply asked me, "Why? What is truly important to you?" Let your life unfold, your passion and purpose lead you to success that you deserve. Hope to meet you soon in Silicon Valley!

Your biggest fan,
—Ari Horie Founder and CEO of Women's Startup Lab

Word from the Author

Marta Zucker holds a Master's degree from Adam Mickiewicz University in Poznan. She began her career in Bucharest building, the Romanian branch of an international company from scratch. She also founded a successful television and film production company in Warsaw. For many years she has worked with the Torun business consulting firm KarStanS Ltd. Marta also consulted independently in New York and San Francisco. For the last five years she has been working with the start-up community in Silicon Valley and in Poland.

From the Author

Global Women in the World of Start-ups: Conversations in Silicon Valley is a continuation of my previous book: "Talent Olympics in Silicon Valley: Conversations with Start-up Masters."

During my author's meeting in Palo Alto at the US-Polish Trade Council, one of my readers asked me why there were no women in *The Olympics of Talents*? Were there only men working in IT? Why did I create an artificial male–female divide? It was purely accidental; however, it is true that the field of new technologies is dominated by men.

Why are there fewer women in senior positions in business and in politics? There are many factors contributing to the fact that women are in the minority among start-up founders.

Although women play a more and more important role at many levels of the economic and political world they still face challenges and difficulties, which can be especially acute in dynamically developing industries where men are the majority of leaders. There is a growing awareness of the tough time facing women in Silicon Valley.

My interviewees are globally minded and strong—they are women who are not afraid of new challenges. The women who are worth following and who deserve to become our role models.

Meet seven ambitious women who consistently achieve their chosen goals, women who are not afraid:

Patrycja Slawuta
Ela Madej
Julia Krysztofiak-Szopa
Amelia Krysztofiak
Kate Scisel
Zuzanna Stańska
Kamila Sidor

My protagonists speak on important topics. They share the stories of their successes and setbacks. They talk about finding their passion and fulfillment in their work. They wonder how to combine the role of a mother with that of an entrepreneur.

There is a saying in Silicon Valley that if a programmer comes to a conference in a dress no one would treat her as a serious partner in conversation. Yet if she wears jeans and a T-shirt we can talk with her about coding. A question arises whether a 21st century programmer working at ground zero of modern technology called Silicon Valley simply cannot be feminine?

The new technology industry is a fantastic place for anyone, male or female, although women there are still in the minority. There are still too few coders, although it is changing. Professional organizations support women and this process seems to spread. Still, it is important for women not to close themselves off in just their own circle. We should promote women not just because they are women but also because they are educated, wise, hardworking, and have passion.

Women often set themselves higher standards than men, they want to be fulfilled not just in their careers but as mothers and it is a difficult feat. What about men who have kids? Let's hope that paternal leave becomes more common.

Is it true that you really *cannot* be a programmer wearing a dress? Let's destroy such myths. With this book I would like to encourage all women and girls to "join the game." The youngest generation of today does not accept artificial division of the world into "pink" and "blue," for toys just for boys or girls. We will not repress their wisdom. As a final note I will cite the words of Van Anh Dam, a mentor in Warsaw and the author of the educational program "Girls Code Fun": "One of our 11-year olds students, after creating her first computer game was asked by journalists who was better at programming—boys or girls. She said she didn't know, as she did not have time to think about it. And that was the best of possible answers."—said Van Anh Dam at the Businesswomen of the Year gala.[1]

***

Thank you to all who helped to make this book happen.

I would also like to thank those individuals who supported this project by donating to the crowdfunding campaign for the book's translation. Your contribution, individually and collectively, is deeply appreciated. All the names are in alphabetical order.

Róża Chojnacka
Lukasz Czerwinski
Maria Duch
Yuka Ioroi
Gosia Kacprzak
Daniel Kindra
Zosia Kostyrko
Sebastian Krawczuk
Ewa Lemanowicz
Mary Beth Stockman
Aldona Woroniecka
Anthony Zukovsky

—Marta Zucker

---

[1] "Bizneswomen Roku nie chcą pomocy od państwa." www.money.pl (accessed February 26, 2016).

CHAPTER 1

SelfHackathon

Breaking the Code of Our Consciousness

Patrycja Slawuta—graduate of the Warsaw University. She studied psychology and sociology. Fellow of the most prestigious science institutions in the United States.

She analyzed aspects of genocide and the psychology of intergroup differences. She researched the emotions of shame, guilt, fear, hate, and animosity between various groups. She worked for two years on Wall Street. Now Patrycja lives in New York and San Francisco.

In Poland she cooperates, among others, with Geek Girls Carrots, an organization supporting women in IT; she participated in Waw.Ac—Warsaw accelerator program and is an active participant of many conferences on technology (ex. Magento.pl).

She is the creator of psychological workshops SelfHackathon, during which she hacks our minds. She cooperates with her sister Joanna Slawuta. Their workshops enjoy enormous popularity in the United States, Europe, South America, and Australia.

Patrycja covers not just human fears, but also long distances—she has run over 18 marathons. She runs all over the world. In near future she will be running in Tokyo, Paris, and Vienna.

We have to turn off the hang-ups. We need to understand how we had been programmed by our environment; whom do we let to program us. Sometimes such programming is toxic and does us harm.

We have to learn to reprogram ourselves, to turn off the brain in some moments and stop listening to critical voices in our heads and "just do it!."

—Patrycja Slawuta

We are meeting on a sunny Monday early in the morning in a coffee shop in San Francisco's Marina neighborhood. Patrycja just moved from New York to the West Coast. She is still fighting jet lag and for the past two days she's been waking up at 4 a.m. "At least I do some more work!" she laughs. She enjoys telling me about her last weekend, when she ran across the Golden Gate Bridge to Sausalito and back—over 18 miles total.

She talks about things that are important for all of us and which we don't want to admit even to ourselves.

Patrycja Slawuta—The slayer of our fears!

About My Research

I conducted lots of research in psychology of extermination and the remembrance of Holocaust in Poland. That was my first research. It was inspired by *Neighbors,* a book by Jan Gross of Yale University. I was interested in the reactions it evolved in Polish people so the subject of my Master's thesis was collective memory in Poland. In my research I describe what actually happened, then what people remember of it and which part they don't and how they selectively remember the facts.

In the fourth year of my studies I went on a scholarship to the Basque Country where I studied the issue of terrorism and its consequences, especially in societies, which directly experienced political violence. I was part of the team studying the complicated psychological and political situation involving the activities of ETA as well as the actions of the Spanish government.

New York

Living in the Basque Country I got news from a colleague of mine from the Warsaw University about a scholarship in New York, for which the application deadline unfortunately had passed... I decided to apply anyway.

Eventually the scholarship was awarded to two people—a young academic from Germany and me. As a research team we received a half a million-dollar grant from the National Science Foundation, one of the most prestigious science foundations in the United States.

The subject of our study was the issue of collective guilt: in particular determining what events lead to the feeling of collective guilt and collective shame. We were looking into issues involving the Guantanamo prison. We analyzed the behavior of people who were reminded that in the past the group to which they belonged had done something bad, committed mass crimes.

After two years of working in academia and writing scientific papers I decided to change my career path and left the university. Although I was passionate about science and research I was more interested in transferring the findings of that research into everyday life.

Wall Street

I chose to change my field. I got a job on Wall Street, where I worked in the years 2009–2010, at the exact time when the world economy was collapsing. I was at ground zero of the crisis. I watched people losing their jobs. I observed the downfall of the giants of the financial world. Those were very important experiences at the intersection of morality, behavioral economy, and anthropology of culture.

The Semantics of Emotions

Still, after two years of working in the financial world I decide to go back to university. I focused on the *embodiment* phenomenon. This is a notion that assumes that abstract concepts and more complex emotions in particular (such as shame) exist not just in the mind but also in the body. It is the semantics of abstraction, which the brain perceives as a sensory experience. For example, love is associated with warmth, softness, and warm colors. Feeling of guilt, on the other hand, involves the feeling of "weight" and the desire to hide from the view of others. Those physiological correlates of emotion are often culturally universal and reflected in colloquial expressions such as "weighed heavy on his heart," "carry the weight of the world on his shoulders." Scientists claim also that the question of embodiment is especially important to all concepts connected with morality. That's why "good" and "evil" often have colloquial equivalents: white and black, high and low, or even left and right.

This is fascinating research, which helps us understand how out internal architecture of beliefs, opinions, and values looks like. This is especially relevant to the world, which is not renowned for its "introspection," since there is simply no time for that—the world of start-ups.

Start-ups

I became interested in the world of start-ups. The world of people who do interesting stuff. How it worked out? I began seeing people who achieved a lot in their lives. They would come to me with their problems and it turned out they needed to talk about their fears, feelings of shame, and experiences of failure, which they did not know how to deal with.

In America facing problems of this kind you get a prescription or go to a yoga class. Yoga of course offers great supports, helps you to calm down and relax. But this is not enough.

The First Workshops

This is the origin of my first workshops. During the meetings we "hack" or "breaking into" our brain and mind.

So far we've held workshops in five countries on three continents, among others, in Poland, Spain, South America, and on both East and West Coasts of the United States.[1] They always sell out, which is encouraging. I cooperate with many companies from all over the world. In Silicon Valley they include the companies in Y Combinator. This year we also "hack" in Asia, which will be an interesting experience, given cultural and social differences.

I do workshops for both women and men. However, the group approach to issues is completely different when I work just with women to when I work with only men. We also often have mixed groups—our workshops attract people who spend a lot of time "in their heads," which to them is both a gift and their greatest curse.

---

[1] Recently also in Australia (Author's note).

SelfHackathon Workshops

Three Main Principles

Principle 1: The Brain Is the Least Discovered Natural Resource

There are all kinds of natural resources such as coal, gold, silver, uranium... However, from the psychological point of view it is the brain and the nervous system that still are the most unexplored and unused natural resource.

Principle 2: We, as Human Beings, Are a Living Code

The sequence of our DNA resembles a code, which changes constantly, just as our nervous connections. The construction of our DNA can be compared to computer code.

It is significant that I have been working with technological companies—programmers code. I get inspired by the similarities in the functioning of our brain and computer code.

Principle 3: The Code Can Be Changed

We know of the neuroplasticity of the brain, which means that the brain changes according to the stimuli received at a given moment. My classes are based on the premise that the code can be broken and changed.

What Would You Like to Hack?

The response is practically always the same. Women usually want to "break into" the spirit of go-getting, self-confidence and man would like to "hack" emotional intelligence. This is why when I work with just men (particularly with programmers) I stress the fundamental elements of emotional intelligence: questions of how to deal with fear and shame. These are the problems not much talked about in Silicon Valley. And unfortunately, in Silicon Valley, the number of people dealing with depression is 40 percent higher than in the rest of the United States. And it is a taboo subject.

Self-Aggression and Self-Sabotage

In Silicon Valley it goes without saying that you should only show the best aspect of yourself, especially if your success is still in the future. I am talking particularly about the process of getting through next rounds of financing by the founders who think that if someone invested in them, if they got the money they have to show more positive energy. Unfortunately sometimes this turns out to be a big problem as their negative emotions don't get any outlet. At one moment they will burst and "scream" to draw attention to themselves.

My work with men consists in talking about ways to deal with emotions. Both positive and negative ones. Men often do not know how to do it.

Women, on the other hand, suffer from low self-esteem, lower feeling of self-worth, and generally lower drive. Women usually take less risk than men and our level of self-criticism is much higher. But Silicon Valley is a new Wild West. It is the capital of risk taking, for which you often get a reward.

Research shows that the level of aggression in both men and women is the same. The difference is that men direct their aggression outwards, women—inwards, apply it to themselves. Various forms of self-aggression and self-sabotage are the two main elements, which I most often address during my classes in Silicon Valley and in New York.

Bro Culture

There is much talk about sexism in Silicon Valley. Personally, I think there was much more sexism on Wall Street than in Silicon Valley.

In the Valley women have to "blend into" to the general coding culture. In San Francisco, more often than in other big cities, you see women wearing sports outfits, guy style. At the same time women complain about the prevalent "bro culture."

There are still relatively few women working in IT. There is even a kind of fascination with women in Silicon Valley. Men who work in IT spend little time with women during their workday, so when they do have a chance to work with a woman they are intrigued and fascinated. In a sense we have a similar situation when men become nurses—sometimes it even causes raised eyebrows.

Differences Between East and West Coast

Women in New York are very aggressive. But New York is an aggressive city.

There is unspoken pressure in New York to always look your best, dress in style, and be in good physical shape. Women are expected to show sophisticated femininity.

I know many men who for their dating go from Silicon Valley to New York because they think women on the East Coast are more feminine, stylish, sexy…

Impostor Syndrome

Women often are scared and don't want to take risks. It is completely understandable given the culture, the social roles, and the potential consequences of "failure." It is a problem I've encountered in every country. Science calls it "impostor syndrome"—it means that we question our own skills; we ask ourselves if we should be where we are, if we should hold this position. It is a common phenomenon in spite of the fact that women do very well at school and in college. More women complete doctorate studies and receive academic degrees.

Yet if we go into business, where many people will judge us, where we have to make decisions, present yourself professionally, where you have to sell yourself—then women become withdrawn or act more cautious.

Internal Limitations

Research shows that woman begin apply for a promotion when they have fulfilled 100 percent the required criteria. Of course this is a sign of redundant perfectionism. Whereas men ask for a promotion when they have just 50–60 percent of fulfilled requirements. Moreover, men negotiate their salaries four times more often while women usually avoid negotiations and if they do negotiate they receive a salary that is 30 percent lower. It is connected with the fact that women generally still earn less than men.

When I started working on Wall Street I was offered a certain salary. Although I knew that people in similar positions earn more I was satisfied with the offer. From our point of view we receive as much as we believe we are worth. We create internal limits as to the money we should be making, how much happiness we should have, how much we can be loved.

First—The Body, Then Motherhood

There are two main factors that activate the feeling of shame in women: first, the body, second—motherhood. The issues involving motherhood always come up in conversations, having children, not having children, being in a relationship, not being in a relationship... We also always encounter comments about female body.

For example, in the situation where a man, probably not intending to create any sexist subtext asks a young woman *When are you planning to have children?* —many women feel embarrassed.

When people ask me such a question I feel I am becoming defensive. Still, this is a popular question asked by the VC representatives in Silicon Valley. It means that the subject of motherhood can have a negative outcome during such an important conversation. We would like to be assessed on the base of what we do and not what we are—mothers, bellies. That's why during talks the question about future motherhood can throw women off.

Ready, Brilliant Answer

The talks with VC people can be viewed as a test of our confidence. The questions are often difficult, detailed, and sometimes even aggressive. Many VCs not often invest in an idea—ideas change all the time, get dropped, are replaced by new ones—but in a person. Investors want to know if we can handle stress and if we are motivated. Will we keep going in spite of difficulties and possible setbacks, which are common in Silicon Valley. When a confident woman comes to a VC meeting, a woman who knows not just her business but also her worth—the conversation will be completely different. In the Wild West called Silicon Valley what matters is courage, confidence, and the ability to present both yourself and your vision of the future.

Comments during such talks can be brutal regardless of the fact if they concern a man or a woman. In this sense gender is irrelevant. The difference is that man has often inflated notion of their worth and are overconfident and if someone tells them *What a stupid idea!*—it will be as water off a duck's back; they will just get up, straighten their clothes, and keep going forward.

Action–Inaction

The feeling of self-worth is a missing element between a dream and action to make it come true. How to rebuild, to reprogram the feeling of self-worth?

Many of us have great ideas but the gap between the world of dreams and realizing them is sometimes too large. Self-esteem or the proactive attitude is the missing element that transforms wishful thinking into something I am actually doing.

The feeling of confidence is connected with action, with "taking matters into your hands." Low self-esteem is connected to passivity, or inaction.

Social Perfectionism

Perfectionism is a character trait. However, there is also something called "social perfectionism."

Many of us are social perfectionists. It means we do not want to start anything at all as it is easier to do nothing than to make something happen. Social perfectionism kills self-esteem because when we do nothing we judge ourselves as less worthy. Social perfectionism comes also from shame. It is easier to do nothing rather than something and be exposed to criticism. A similar behavior is procrastination.

Three Major Elements of Programming

Every day 60 to 80 thoughts cross our minds. Ninety percent are repetitive thoughts, always the same.

People like to believe that they think what they want. Unfortunately this is not true. Usually we think of something we heard or read. This is how we had been culturally programmed.

During my workshops I always speak about three major elements of programming: **Thoughts, Heart, and Environment.**

First Element—Thoughts

First—the head, our thoughts. What do we think about? How do we view the world?

Einstein said that the fundamental question was not if God existed or not but whether the Universe was friendly or not. And this is the fundamental question: do we believe that people are friendly and want to help us, a kind of "positive conspiracy" or maybe we think that the world is evil and people want to take advantage of us?

For a while I had been "negatively programmed." In my "software" there was a red light that kept coming on: *Watch out! See what they are doing behind your back! Be careful as THEY will steal your ideas, your business!* It took me a few years to reprogram myself.

It turns out other people don't busy themselves thinking about us too much, neither do they "plot" to "get us" or defeat us.

Determining if the world is friendly or not, if people want to help us or not we often assume that humanity operates on the principle of trading favors. This is one of the fundamental programs, filters through which we view the world. In truth people help others because of their giving nature. Human nature is good if one's let it be that way.

What We Think About Ourselves—What Is My Worth?

Limiting Beliefs

These are false beliefs that I always mention during my classes. There are three kinds of limiting beliefs:

1. I am fundamentally broken

Statistics are terrifying—many of us have an "internal critics" in our heads—voices, which live in our minds are internalized judgments someone had once made about us, or demonstrated with their behavior. Those voices have been coded into us. Especially women are prone to internal such self-criticism.

2. I am unlovable

We are convinced that we have to hide the truth about ourselves as there is "something" wrong with the way we are. That's why we don't deserve love, intimacy, and acceptance.

3. I am a failure

Giving up without a fight. Perseverance, patience, and the ability to pick yourself up after failure are the fundamental elements of success not just in Silicon Valley, but in general.

Such thoughts often hide deep in our subconscious. They are hard to pinpoint and in order to get rid of them sometimes we need to reprogram our personality.

Where Do These Thoughts Come From?

All the way from our childhood; from our experiences; from what we once heard, saw, and lived through.

It takes one experience for us to start looking at the world through a "filter." As a result we create a self-fulfilling prophecy. We need to understand the way we have been programmed to be able to deprogram ourselves. Some people are culturally programmed. I often work with people from Asia where they have a completely different "programming," one stemming from their culture.

Research shows that until age 25 we get programmed by the environment—school, culture, and parents. If after 25 we don't start reprogramming ourselves we are operating on "old software."

What to Do? Think Differently

First we have to realize we have limiting beliefs. Next we need to understand where they came from. Oftentimes when we look back we are able to recall details or events from our life that made a given thought program itself in a certain way. Sometimes it is by pure accident.

When I was 12 I was laughed at because I was wearing a dreadful tracksuit. I still remember it clearly. Such events become deep memories. Sometimes they are so painful that we forget about them or reject them.

Still, in spite of the passage of time, they keep subconsciously influencing our lives. As a result for years we tell ourselves: *don't dress different than others or else you will be ridiculed again.* That's why we have to start with consciousness. Zen philosophy and Buddhism also want you to be aware of your thoughts so that you can track down their origin. Nature abhors vacuum. That's why we cannot just reject our thoughts and tell ourselves: *I will no longer think this way.* We have to slowly change the interpretation of that event and start to think about ourselves in a new way.

How to Change My Thinking?

Three Aspects—ABC: Affective, Behavioral, and Cognitive

We change our thoughts **on the affective level: we change our emotions.**

Many women when asked if they liked themselves said they did not. This is quite shocking.

Asked *if they were someone else they would like to spend time with themselves?* They also say they wouldn't, they would not enjoy meeting themselves. Our attitude toward ourselves, the answer to the question why we do not like ourselves are issues studied by Stanford scientists, looking at women's empathy toward themselves.

Women don't have empathy for themselves.

We often empathize with others, but not with ourselves. We scorn ourselves for doing something wrong, something stupid again: *you had another chocolate!* Such thinking is not rooted in good self-esteem.

Behavioral Aspect or How to Change our Behavior

For example, when we never talk to anyone at meetings the brain receives this message: *I act this way because I am an introvert.*

Yet if we do something against our old habits and the situation forces us to start a conversation then we get another feedback, which questions our assertion that we are introverted.

These are the baby steps, which involve feedback and result in changes in our behavior.

Cognitive Aspect—Mind and Thoughts

This is very interesting insight—understanding what events made someone hold certain beliefs about oneself. Understanding the role of a woman
and of a man. You can see then that some of our thoughts are completely
absurd and irrational. This is like an anthropological study of ourselves,
how we behave, what we say.

Viktor Frankl said that between the stimulant (the way someone acts
toward us) and the response (the way we react) there is a space where we
can make a choice. This is the space where our humanity operates. One-
third of a second might pass before we respond to a stimulus. Often we
react automatically, as if on autopilot. This is why it is considered that 90
percent of our thoughts are repetitive. We repeat the same thoughts and
respond with the same thoughts, the same behavior.

Second Element—Heart

The second element is the heart, or the emotions, both positive and negative ones. This aspect connects to the rather unpopular feeling of shame
and many kinds of fears.

Male and female brains have the same amount of neurons, the same
number of neural connections. This is undisputed. The female skull is
smaller because a woman's body is smaller. The proportions of male and
female bodies are identical. Some parts of female brain gets easily acti-
vated—as for instance the limbic system and the amygdala, connected to
the fight or flight response.

Women ruminate a lot, which means they more often consider various solutions, commiserate, think of possible outcomes. We can wonder
a whole night why we did what we did. To end rumination is to get "out
of your head," so movement and action. And the first step toward this is
realizing that thoughts self-propel.

Men have an easier time admitting to a mistake: *I failed, I did it wrong.*
Next time I will do better. Women are taught to do things perfectly—we
don't make mistakes and if we do they reflect on us as people. Failure
often paralyzes and blocks us from taking further action.

That's why our goal is to focus on action. Sometimes we have to turn off the thinking part of the brain and just do something. Brain is like a muscle that can be easily trained.

We need to learn to exchange rumination into action.

Third Element—Environment

The third element is the environment. Surroundings versus "SELF."

Neurological research carried out at UCLA indicate that there is no such thing as "Self." The "Self" is made up of information received from others, from the outside world. Our "Self" is the result of all those influences. What we consider our SELF is made up of the thoughts heard from my mother, my husband, my grandmother, anyone with whom I spend my time. This is why it is so important to decide whom we allow to program us. There is a grain of truth in the saying that we are the median of five people with whom we spend our time. I have seen this in myself. When I am in Poland I am a different person because different people influence me there.

Because of this it is important to pay attention to who is our "social model." Whose behavior we copy, in whose footsteps we follow. And are we doing it consciously or not.

Social Support

My dad says that when you make a fire in a stove you have to first make the draft in the chimney. When you have the draft the fire burns by itself.

Today we women, especially in IT, are building this "draft" together. One pulls another up. There is no space for envy, competition as in "if she gets it, there will not be enough for me." There is lots of money available on the market. Thinking that "there won't be enough for me" is old typo of thinking which doesn't help anyone.

When I worked on Wall Street I observed how men were helping each other out, how they "pulled each other up," supported one another.

It is only recently that women gave themselves permission for such cooperation, for mutual support. We celebrate our friend's success without assuming that since she managed to do it, I will not. Such thinking is fear-based and connected to the thought "I will not make it in time" —I will not manage to have a child, I will not manage to get a career. You don't have to rush everything so much, be scared that there won't be enough for us. We are living in the times of plenty and of unprecedented historical peace.

When We Are Our Own Enemy

Women sometimes try to shame other women using it as means of control. Girls who have issues around their bodies shame other women because it is easier to vent your aggression on another woman. This is very toxic. This kind of bullying starts with ourselves and this is why it is so important to have compassion for oneself. Only then you can begin to feel empathy for another. Artificial "niceness" is easily felt. Unfortunately, sometimes we are our own worst enemies.

Can Women Give Themselves Credit?

Women don't brag. This is very sad. During my workshops I teach women to boast of their successes, even the smallest ones. We don't boast because we are afraid of envy, shame, we are afraid to say something inappropriate. Women often say "I was lucky" which means that their success was not the result of their hard work but was due only to luck. Sometimes this is not true, as we work very hard.

Women think in a more social way. We like to talk with our friends, but do we just gossip or do we talk about our successes? To reprogram those conversations is an interesting and worthwhile challenge.

During my workshops we create groups in which the participants have to praise themselves for something. Even for just going out to a yoga class. These are everyday matters yet for me they build the feeling of being in a group of women with whom I can share my successes and I know that they will listen and understand me.

In one of my groups I had some famous people. The change that occurred in their self-assessment was incredible. Before they started they were afraid to say they were on CNN or that they got an award in Cannes. They didn't think much of it. To be able to give yourself credit for what you've done is a natural, but paradoxically it does not come naturally to us.

Let's pat ourselves on the back! Maybe even for small things, such as a dinner with your husband: *It was a busy day but I want to congratulate myself for spending a nice evening with my husband.*

Femininity—A New Trend?

There is a new trend focusing on anything concerning women. This is a good direction as many women do interesting things.

These days both in New York and in Warsaw there are many meetings, conferences and workshops for women. I am not sure if the gatherings for just women will be better than the mixed ones. Research shows that creativity needs diversity.

Still, some matters should be discussed just among women. When we talk about the feeling of shame involving our bodies or our motherhood—these subjects are so intimately feminine that the male participation could affect the comfort level of participants. Statistics shows that when men are present women's participation in the discussion falls by 75 percent. That's why it's important to create a safe space for conversation.

It happened to me in my professional life that I had the answers but did not speak up. Someone else did. Later, on my way home, I asked myself why I remained silent.

Public Speaking

Women who speak up in public are less liked, since they are perceived as arrogant, aggressive in their behavior, and pushy. Research shows that the audience doesn't like women who are the first ones to state their opinion. On the other hand if we never say anything we disappear in the crowd. So we walk a thin line and it is easy to fall.

Sometimes a question arises: can we deal with the situation when someone accuses us of being arrogant and pushy?

A person with a healthy self-esteem would answer: *Yes, I am courageous and I am the first one to speak.*

Or do we prefer to keep quiet and later feel bad about saying nothing?

Change has to come from within and without—both in the environment and in women's consciousness.

Research shows that women have an easier time speaking if they represent not just themselves but a larger group of women. We prefer to say: "In our opinion…" instead of "In my opinion…" We speak then on behalf of a group of women.

The More Diverse the Group, the More Creative It Is

It is a known fact that mixed social groups are more creative. Diversity increases creativity. This is why there is so much discussion about the presence of women in the field of technology. It turns out that the meetings are much more fruitful when there are women participants. Their voice makes it possible to introduce another point of view on many issues that so far have only been discussed by men. This goes another way too—at a meeting where only women are present the male perspective might be lacking.

There is a growing awareness in the United States that many business incubators or accelerators have only *white women* participation. So this is the issue of not just gender, but also ethnic diversity. What if there were more women from Asia, more African American or Latinos? We are taking first steps to improve this ratio, but there is much to be done.

To Kill an Idea Is the Easiest Thing

The same parts of the brain that are responsible for physical pain are involved in perceiving social pain and the pain of rejection. That's why being ostracized hurts physically. We all fear rejection. We are scared someone will say "no," someone will say our idea is hopeless.

These situations are very common in the start-up world.

That's why the companies who get into Y Combinator for the first three months, during the incubation, close themselves off from any external influence. New ideas are so vulnerable that they require special protection.

Such was the case when AirBnb was a start-up. The idea was questioned; people wondered *Who would want to sleep on a mattress in a stranger's home?* Today Airbnb is worth several billion dollars. However, the idea was so sensitive and fragile that for three months it had to stay in an incubator.

This is the origin of the name "business incubator" since it shelters young ideas from external influences.

Because it is the easiest thing to kill and ridicule ideas. And, unfortunately, there are many societies where negative criticism is a "national sport," where it is common practice to call any new idea ridiculous and dismiss it with *What is she thinking? Who does she thinks she is?*

Male Start-ups—Female Start-ups

In comparison to the start-ups created by men, women founded start-ups stay longer on the market enjoying success. "Male" start-ups quickly get going and climb up. "Female" start-ups take more time. It looks a bit like motherhood and taking care of a baby.

A Professionally Fulfilled Mom?

When people start having children both a woman and a man become more conservative in their roles of a mother or a father. This is regardless how liberal both people were before.

Are mothers who stay at home with their children unhappy?

Many women love to take care of children and give up their careers to take care of the family. Many others, however, are unhappy that they had to put their professional life aside. Some of my clients are women who left their jobs, sit at home and suffer. Others were able to combine their home duties with careers. These situations again involve the feelings of shame as this is not just about work but also about self-image: what kind of mother I am, what others think about me. Women think that if they continue to work they will be bad mothers. In spite of the known fact that daughters of working mothers do better in adult life. Working mothers are often more productive and better organized than working women who don't have kids.

A friend of mine is a mother of a three-month old, keeps working, and does well at her job. Such approach is encouraging and should be followed.

In the United States more and more men stay at home to take care of the children. The model of the American family is changing, especially here, in Silicon Valley.

Will it be easier in the future to combine the roles of a mother and a working woman? I don't have the answer.

Maternity Leave—In Poland or in the United States?

In the United States maternity leave is unpaid and lasts only three months.[2] Many women think that the first three months of being a mom are the hardest. Taking care of a newborn is hard, time consuming and exhausting. When the child begins to be more fun, begins to communicate, a woman must return to work to pay for a nanny… At that moment the vicious circle begins as her whole income goes into paying for child care.

In Poland I met many young women who during their paid maternity leave started their own business. They say that it helped their companies to take off.

Changing Role of Man

I know some men whom you interviewed for your book "Talent Olympics in Silicon Valley: Conversations with Start-up Masters" and I know that they take care of their children and at the same time are really successful. They can be real role models for other couples.

The role of a man in raising children and is very important. The myth that only the mother takes care of the children is fading. Unfortunately the stereotypical "Polish Mothers," women who sacrificed everything for the sake of the family, had a negative impact on the future of their children.

A new trend arises and the role of men in the lives of children is changing. It is happening in both Warsaw and the Silicon Valley. Some men are not quite happy about it, as women are becoming stronger. Still, there are others who enjoy the new situation and they appreciate the increased professional activity of women. Still, many feel threatened. It is

---

[2] Except for modern technology firms such as Google, YouTube, Facebook, and so on, which slowly change this practice.

reflected in lame, sexist comments publicly expressed by some men. It is their defense mechanism since they fear the loss of their power, status, and role.

What Does It Mean to Be a Woman, a Man?

Traditional roles begin to change. What will the new woman, the new man be like? How will their new roles be formed?

In the United States homosexual couples can marry. Gender definitions are becoming less rigid. What does it mean to be a woman or a man? We can already say that although physically I am a woman I choose for myself another gender. I will follow my own plan and I will be the person I want to be. I can run marathons, create companies, and take risky decisions. The question is not "Why?" but "Why not?"

Power Couples

Nowadays we stop talking about *a power man* or *a power woman* but we begin to talk about *power couples.* In the United States creative couples are becoming trendy. When two influential people come together and create something important, introduce changes, they become a modern power couple. A new unit is being created, a unit made up of two strong, influential people. You can see such couples on the political and business world—for example, Barack and Michelle Obama or Bill and Melinda Gates. The women do not hide in the shadow of their husbands but are professionally active, at the same time remaining very feminine. And these people are perceived not necessarily as individuals but as a pair that creates something together.

In Poland there are also some interesting role models, although there the changes take more time. I know many Polish couples who travel with their children. They put the kids in their backpacks and go for a month to Mexico... I hope there will be more families like that.

My Advice—Just Do it!

My motto has always been *Just do it!*

This saying has an interesting history. It is a Nike slogan heard from a runner from New Hampshire.

The story goes like this:

One of Nike employees would see a jogger who did his running every day, even in the snow or during a rain storm. He just stepped out and ran.

Finally the employee asked him: *How do you do it? The sky is falling and you run!*

The runner replied: *Just do it!*

So this is how the slogan came up.

You have to turn off your hang-ups. You have to understand whom you let program you. Sometimes the programming is very toxic.

You have to learn how to reprogram yourself, when to turn off your brain and stop listening to the critical voices in your head and: *Just do it!*

Do not fear...

I heard this advice many times. It keeps coming back in my life. I don't know if it is fate... but people often tell me not to be afraid. Just like that.

I heard it first from an old woman in a Mexican village. She said: *Do not fear.* Consciously, I had no idea what she was talking about. Subconsciously I understood her very well. This is what I sometimes tell myself: *Do not fear.*

Fears exist only in the mind.

So, girls—*Do not fear.*

This is my message to you.

***

The interview took place July 6, 2015 in San Francisco.

CHAPTER 2

Fifty Years

In Pursuit of Better Tomorrow

Ela Madej, the founder of Applicake, Base CRM, and Credictive. Partner in the Krakow investment fund Innovation Nest. Co-founder of California fund Fifty Years. Longtime supporter of Polish start-up community. Graduate of the prestigious Y Combinator accelerator. With her start-up Credictive, a part of the first Polish team to be accepted to Y C.

She comes from Krakow. She lived on both the East and the West Coast of the United States. Recently she moved back to Silicon Valley.

Ela's professional journey in brief:

2006—Krakow: Applicake software house
2009—Krakow: start-up Base CRM, Hive53 community, EuRuKo and Railsberry conferences
2012—Silicon Valley: Y Combinator accelerator; start-up Credictive
2014—New York: Innovation Nest fund; start-up Amicus
2015—Silicon Valley: Fifty Years Fund, impact.tech community

Many very clever people create companies just for profit. This doesn't really solve the most important problems such as unequal access to resources, public health etc. People in the start-up field have incredible intellectual potential. However, the goals they choose are not too sophisticated—interesting from the business point of view but not too smart in from the viewpoint of the rest of humanity. I was troubled by that.

—Ela Madej

I asked Ela to tell me what she was doing today and to develop on the successes and failures of her start-ups, founded over the last 10 years. I also heard from her about start-up ecosystems in New York and Silicon Valley. She gives valuable, mature advice not just to young people but to anyone wondering about choosing their career path and anyone caring about the future of our planet. She considers many aspects of running a start-up. Conversation with her is an intellectual analysis of today's world largely influenced by Buddhist philosophy.

I met with Ela in San Francisco's SoMa district (South of Market).

In the 1990s, SoMa underwent an economic transformation connected to the dotcom boom.

Today SoMa is populated by many people from the start-up community, new technologies, IT and host the headquarters of some of the smartest tech companies such as Instacart and Airbnb.

The First Steps

The First Company—Applicake

In 2006, with my friends Paweł Niżnik, Bartek Kiszala, and Agata Mazur we created Applicake—we were creating software in Ruby on Rails technology. I was in my second year of college.

The story began when Paweł went for training to a Stockholm company Edulab where he learned Ruby on Rails technology. After he returned to Poland the Swedes invited him to cooperate. In Krakow, Pawel gathered a group of friends; I was going to help manage the company. I did not see my future in this. I just wanted to help my friends and in a few months go my own way. We decided to have equal shares in the company. It wasn't always easy, but Applicake began to grow. From the very beginning we worked with start-ups, mostly from abroad.

Naive Attempts

Soon we decided to create something independently. Today I can say our first efforts were naive. We tried to create games and social networks, one of them was a service called tripy.pl. Honestly, we really did not know what we were doing... There was very little chance for those projects to succeed. It does happen that such things like games and social networks sites take off but usually it is just by luck on accident. We didn't make it but we had a lot of fun!

Base

We decided to start organizing meetings for the programmers of Ruby language and the Rail framework. We also started to organize large conferences. We became recognizable on the European technological stage.

In 2009, we got a letter from Uzi Shmilovici, today's CEO of Base CRM company. He said he had an interesting idea that he wanted to start and invited us to cooperate. We refused. It was supposed to be work-for-shares and our principle was not to take on such projects: many start-ups use such strategy to avoid financial risk. It is a difficult business model for software houses.

Uzi was insistent—finally he convinced us and we began to work together. This was the beginning of Base CRM which is doing the best of all the companies I had been involved in. (Nota Bene without me!) In time Base CRM took over Applicake. Today it employs 170 people. It is based in Mountain View in Silicon Valley, an office in San Francisco and a strong programming team in Krakow. They are doing great.

So those were our beginnings.

Hive53

Applicake was bootstrapped, so created with our own money and developed from the profits. Our next projects were also financed from the cash flow.

Start-ups were our clients a few years ago, when people didn't really know what a start-up was. That's why Piotrek Nędzyński and I created Hive53 start-up community. Now it is being run by the next generation of entrepreneurs, which makes me very happy.

For the Love of Kracow...

I love Krakow; I was born there, I grew up there and went to school, this is where I have many friends, my family lives there. This is a kind of feeling you have for your own child. I like the rhythm of life in Krakow—much less stressful than the United States. I like the atmosphere of the city, the art scene—theaters, indie cinemas. I like Cracovian slow foods and crossing the town square on my bike. I moved out of Krakow a while ago but I always love to go back.

Krakow attracts and educates many clever and technically savvy programmers. In the Krakow start-up ecosystem we have more and more local successes that become global successes, such as Base CRM, Estimote, Seedlabs, Brainly. There are several investment funds located in Krakow, such as Innovation Nest. Of course you cannot compare it to the IT in Silicon Valley but Krakow does have a few global companies. We are cheering for the next ones.

Y Combinator

Credictive

We got into Y Combinator as the first company from Poland with the idea for Credictive. Generally it was "all great" but many things we could have been done better. We wanted to accelerate a product, which required more time and product-market-fit research. For me, as a CEO, everything was too crazy and stressful. Inside the team there was also pressure to focus on just one thing. Just before Demo Day I finally decided to call off the funding round that was already on the way, although we had interest from investors such as Andreessen Horowitz.

Why the Investors Liked Us?

The founders of Y Combinator did not like Credictive, they cared more about our great team and maybe my personal "charisma" played a small part. Paul Graham seemed to like me, although it might be too warm a word for it. From the very beginning they wanted us to work on something else. It was a kind of anti-support.

Andreessen Horowitz, on the other hand, liked Credictive, as we were trying to create a tool for meta tagging Internet items for their attribution, meaning the people who contributed to the creation of certain content. You might compare our product to movie credits. We talked to Creative Commons and people from Wikipedia, among others.

I think the time for Credictive type product is still in the future but someone has to do it without pressure. After this episode we decided to put all our energy to Base CRM.

Too Early

Many start-ups got accepted to our edition, including our Credictive, that should never have gone there. We got there too early. I had no way of knowing that but people from YC should have foreseen it. We were only just finishing a product and after the accelerator we were supposed to be ready for financing. That was a bit crazy.

Most founders who try to get into YC observe YC and Paul Graham for many months or even years. Myself, I never felt that YC was such a special place. When I learned about it I thought it was worth trying because the accelerator offers good financial terms and we wanted to develop our product and "learn" Silicon Valley.

Accelerator Is an Investment Fund

At that stage I was not aware that Y Combinator was an accelerator, not an incubator. An accelerator for its three month program tries to maximally speed up start-ups of a given batch, regardless of the level of their development. If a team does not yet have a specific vision of their product there is a chance that such accelerated "development" might be too rapid. Accelerator is an investment fund that aims at quickly developing companies it takes on. Even if only a few of those companies will stay on the market and only 5 percent of them will grow into robust corporations, mathematically speaking this business model makes sense. In reality, the sooner the remaining companies collapse the better, as they don't need to to be taken care of anymore.

Y Combinator—My Experience

Looking back I think that being in Y Combinator was a positive experience. I maintain many connections that started there. I think I understood better how Silicon Valley works—unlike what most people imagine it's less about the hype, more about hard business.

Thanks to participating in YC I became clear about how I would like to work in my future. My previous work routine, although developed over six years, did not work at YC. I think the work style in Silicon Valley is not always "healthy."

This year 7,000 start-ups applied to Y Combinator. The majority are well-established companies making some profit. About a 100 gets accepted into the program.

"Island Under the Rainbow"

For people in the start-up field going through an accelerator is like getting an MBA. In YC I learned about how the ecosystem of start-ups and investors really work. That knowledge turned out to be quite valuable for me. Without it I would not be able to do what I do now. Before getting into YC I lived in an idealized world, a bit on an "island under the rainbow." That's why the new, pragmatic approach to reality was for sure helpful.

New York vs. Silicon Valley

Escape from Silicon Valley

When we finished the YC program I left Silicon Valley. I didn't want to be here, I did not feel at home in the strictly techy environment, after getting my ass kicked at YC. In Silicon Valley most conversations deal with start-ups and technology. I had a feeling the human element was overlooked. Maybe we, Europeans, especially those from Eastern Europe have a great need for communities, not necessarily goal oriented.

In Krakow I was busy co-organizing the Railsberry conference. At that time Applicake was finally taken over by Base CRM.

New York

In later years my life took me to New York where the start-up scene is also very interesting. During my stay there I decided—partly for personal reasons—to do something different, although I did not know exactly what it would be. I decided that having worked really hard for last seven years I deserved a longer holidays—a sabbatical. I decided to give some thought to what I should do and would like to do. I needed a break. With my friend Socha we left for two months for Argentina and after returning to the United States I signed up for a three—month course of modern dance at a Broadway school. Finally I decided to stay in New York.

New York Technology Scene

It is relatively easy to get to know the New York start-up-technology environment. Every month there is a NYTech Meetup—an event bringing together people from most technology fields. This is where you can start getting to know the New York IT environment. There are also two renowned and influential newsletters: Charlie O'Donnell's and Gary Sharmy's.

Industries of New York

New York is not such as homogenous place as Silicon Valley. There are some coexisting fintech ecosystems (financial technology), practically the whole financial technology industry with their own meet-ups and conferences. The industry is pretty much all financed by Wall Street investors who watch closely the trends of technological-financial innovation. There is also adtech (advertisement and technology), e-commerce, and biotech. Quite large publishing and fashion industries are also located in New York. Most of those industries—except for maybe some branches of biotech—is, for my taste, too much focused on generating profit.

I spent a few difficult months looking for a place for myself and decided I still have to look further.

Multicultural City

For a Polish start-up it is easier to begin in New York. First, the time difference is only six hours, not nine, compared to Silicon Valley. It means that if you have teams in both the United States and Poland communication is easier. Besides, New York is not as expensive as Silicon Valley and is much more culturally diverse. It is probably also easier to find employees in New York—it has more people from a variety of industries. New York start-up ecosystem is also very mature—second in the world, just after

Silicon Valley. Brainly, Estimote, and some other Polish start-ups already have their offices in NYC.

Finally, although no more of critical importance, New York has a large Polish diaspora. So if we crave *barszcz* or *pierogi* we can go to Greenpoint, the traditional Polish neighborhood which is now transforming into a cool, hipster zone. It is worth visiting.

Hip vs. Stylish

Compared to Silicon Valley New York is more worldly and European, which can be felt also in the start-up community.

New York start-ups sometimes resemble large, genuine business run by young people. At fintech meetings in San Francisco we will not meet men in white shirts. In New York people in the financial or advertising business wear business suit and sometimes overdress. Designer shoes, expensive clothes are in. This is not exactly my world.

In San Francisco and especially in Silicon Valley people are more at ease. Practically no one dresses up; the key is comfort. This works for me.

The Culture of Activity

New York is a vast city with distances between some neighborhoods similar to those between Katowice and Krakow. Living in New York you have to schedule every meeting in advance since a simple visit at friends at the other end of the city means a long trip.

San Francisco is smaller and more community minded. Wonderful weather and the location in proximity of national parks, beaches, and mountains encourage weekend trips to the country. People go to the vineyards in Napa Valley. Generally they spend more time together, off work. Active outdoor lifestyle is a large part of the culture of San Francisco.

New York—New Challenges

More Than Just Work...

I spent less than a year in New York. I contacted all the entrepreneurs and investors that I knew and asked them for "intros" for their social networks. There was a month when I had five, six meetings a day. It was very exhausting but I learned a lot. I did not know yet my game plan but I wanted to meet and talk. I got to know many interesting companies and some of them I was even able to help. I knew I was neither interested in the role of co-founder in a new start-up nor in being an analyst in a larger fund. I wondered what could I do so that my everyday activity would not be just work. I was always drawn to science and real innovation. I made a list of science—technology start-ups active in New York and I met with their founders. Simultaneously I was in advanced talks with an interesting educational start-up and was considering joining them as a VP of Sales. I also had an offer to join a large start-up Trello, also in VP position. I also got another great offer but I am not supposed to talk about it. Those were offers of senior roles in well-developed companies. At the end of the day I decided not to join an unknown team. I also did not want to be just an employee. Maybe it is my elevated ego speaking but I knew it would be hard for me to assimilate in that role. I was concerned someone would limit my creativity.

Innovation Nest Fund

At that time I started talking with Piotr Wilam, who encouraged me to join the Innovation Nest Fund. The Fund already had a presence in the United States but Piotr wanted to expand the scope of its activity. I, on the other hand, was more interested in working with people. Innovation Nest team is based in Krakow, which meant I would be working in the States all by myself. Eventually we worked out an arrangement, which enabled me to spend a few months a year in Krakow. An interesting window into learning the nuts and bolts of the investment world opened up for me.

We worked together for a few months and it was a great experience. I really appreciate what Piotr, Marek, and Marcin are doing.

Amicus

In the meantime I noticed that in start-up Amicus, funded by my partner Seth Bannon, they needed a managerial help. Amicus is a social good start-up creating software for large nonprofit organizations. I wondered if I should step in and help them… Finally I joined Amicus part time as a Chief Operating Officer while continuing to work for Innovation Nest. This was the beginning of yet another (sic!) "most intensive time in my life." And since I took up that challenge I wanted to carry through. That's probably why I quickly lost heart for New York. The months I spend in the city were among the hardest in my life, considering the level of stress and responsibility.

Seth tried twice to fire me to give me some respite. I did not let him.

From the Investor Viewpoint

Grand Scheme of Things

At the same time I was ready to make another decision, this time involving my position as an investor. I like working with start-ups; investing in young companies is very interesting. Yet as an investor I held an uncomfortable position—I thought that start-ups were redundant. Many very smart people create companies just for profit and later struggle with it. Maybe because they seemingly "change the world" but in fact they don't solve any serious problems such as suffering, hunger, or unfair access to resources. People involved in the start-up industry have enormous intellectual capital, yet the goals they set for themselves are mediocre—interesting from the business point of view but mundane in the grand scheme of things. I began to worry about it.

A Story for an Investor

Start-ups are an uncertain venture. That's why VC financing for companies at the very early stage of their development is a relatively new model in Poland. Not only because there was a long break in capitalism in Poland. Traditionally companies look for investors only when they already have started turning a profit and want to expand, or when they have no profit but they can somehow predict it. Start-ups on the other hand are companies with great potential but by definition still searching for their business model. Today many companies, following Silicon Valley example look for an investor when all they have is a crazy idea.

Start-ups particularly those in Silicon Valley created a complex ecosystem. Part of it is the network of investors ready to support the creativity of people who devoted many years of their lives to something very uncertain in order to create something new. And they need a lot of capital for it.

Often we create a whole selling story for the benefit of investors, where we describe out team, our vision and explaining why we are likely to be successful. This story is essential especially when the company is in the early stage. To tell people that we will make it we have to believe it ourselves. We persuade ourselves and others that that particular project represents our life mission. It must be so since we devote 10 years of our life to it being aware that there is an over 90 percent chance it will fail. This is very tough on the psyche, especially for young people. I have a big problem with that. I think someone's life mission can be finding a cure for cancer but creating a better website that will retarget users to another websites to buy things they don't need for the money they don't have is not a life mission.

Locked Up in the Cage of Projects

When a company is bootstrapped the founders can have in a way an easy attitude to their operation. Connecting with investors changes that. Often it can be a very constructive relationship but it involves creating a special way of communicating. We start playing certain roles. The founders, usually young people, don't realize that creating stories—partly for the investors, partly for the press, partly for themselves—they create around themselves a layer of identity, which is not always true and certainly not complete. The mythologization which follows closes us in a kind of cage, limits us; we become prisoners to the part of our identity we created. I know many people that locked themselves into the cages they had made.

On Start-ups

Most Start-ups Fail

Among start-up founders there are many young people, this is characteristic of IT industry. Young people are experts on new technologies, they can code, they follow trends, are not afraid of risk, and can afford long periods of unsalaried work. Usually they also have some kind of vision and/or mission and take up the challenge to build and maintain a team.

So we talk about a good "founder material," someone who needs to be courageous and original enough to choose a less traveled path. Especially, that at the beginning they have to face huge lack of support. Sometimes we make great plans, which might not be feasible. We sell our vision, which, according to many, cannot come true.

There is a whole question of stress in the start-up industry. Until recently the episodes of depression or even suicides in the start-up world were not talked about. Maybe there was not sufficient data. Recently TechCruch writes more and more about this problem.

A kind of ideology emerged around the star-ups, which suggests that creating start-ups "we change the world for the better." It is a strange ideology. Especially, given that the number of companies that are successful or those that do something good for humanity oscillates is close to a standard error—the majority of companies never succeed. Not to mention that from all the masses of beginning start-ups only 5–10 percent manage to survive on the market. Most people feed their dreams reading about virtual or real successes of others.

What Does Matter for Us and What Are Our Priorities?

It is important to know why we are doing this. From the mathematical standpoint it is better to find a good job in a corporation because "entrepreneurship" is not a sure way to make money. After calculating what percent of star-ups can reach high value it is best to join one after it got financing in round A or B and work for already reasonable pay and for shares that might be worth something. As entrepreneurs we usually pay ourselves very little in the first years. Eventually it might turn out that it doesn't work. That's why it is so important to ask ourselves these questions: Why am I doing this? What are my priorities? Our time is precious.

Creating Something of Your Own

For people who value freedom, have a concrete vision to realize, and feel ill at ease in the corporate world working for start-ups is a good solution.

Maybe I should not comment on that since I've never worked for a corporation. I don't know this world. I had three co-founders—two men and one woman and together we built a team where we were all equals and had the same powers. But it was a small company. So let's leave corporations aside. I like to create new things. Jus founding an organization is already creative act for me. I also like to be in control so my own business is perfect for me! :)

Mindfulness in Organizations

Leadership is built mostly through hard work, communication with the team and—in longer perspective—making good business decisions. A leader can perform many roles and does not have to stop being a colleague in a team.

Often you think of IT professionals as people who are very analytical, who need to be addressed in a short, concise way. This is not true. Managing intelligent people you need to use more empathy since when team members share common understanding the communication is smooth. I recommend the book *Mindfulness In Organizations*. Mindfulness for me is an intriguing way of living and approaching life.

Timing

In the start-up founding team people and culture are the most important elements. Still, for success the most important factor is timing, the moment we enter the market. A lot depends on us, but at the same time just as much is out of our control. Over 90 percent of star-ups fail not because the teams were not smart enough but because they entered the market at the wrong time. Sometimes an idea is excellent, but it catches on two years later.

When We Fail

Silicon Valley is forgiving toward failure. Here people take on enormous challenges, which involve even greater risks. On the surface it seems easier, but still many people cannot handle failure—they go into an emotional slump. Some leave for few months to regenerate. I have been there. But then they come back stronger.

I don't know if it is possible to avoid failure. When we disbanded Credictive I felt we closed an unfinished project. It was very hard on me. We were solvent but even so we decided to close the company. We finished our operation not because it was not possible to go on, but because we did not want to go on. I asked myself many times if it was the right decision. I still think it was. But it was hard.

The first failure is probably the hardest. Ending Credictive was my first failure. I shall see how it goes and how I will deal with the next one. Statistically there are a few more "fails" ahead.

When Things Fall Apart

When we do something that requires full commitment from us we tell ourselves that our work is worth our dedication and time. We get very emotionally involved. I, for that matter, take what I do very personally. I can't keep my distance without losing interest at the same time. That's why it is so important to work out a system of dealing with failure. I was greatly helped by *When Things Fall Apart*, a book by Pemy Chodron. The book explains the Buddhist perspective of dealing with change. When we build a part of our personality over something very important to us and later that part no longer exists we feel lost. I personally experienced a hard lesson and the "rebuilding" from scratch when at one moment many aspects of my life changed. When many variables of our identity transform all at once we have to learn to build ourselves anew.

Silicon Valley Take Two

Life Decision

Many people come to Silicon Valley hoping for success. But Silicon Valley is a tough place to make it. Living here you might get an impression that everybody is happy to talk to you, but those conversations might not lead anywhere. The competition is just very strong.

When I moved to Silicon Valley for the second time in May 2015, I had already been here a number of times. It seems to me that anyone who plans to move to Silicon Valley should first visit it several times. This is why Innovation Nest fund brings founders here before they are ready to make the move. Some never decide to live in Silicon Valley. It is a tough life decision, affecting the rest of our career. Before moving here for good you should ask yourself why do it, what is so special about it? Although I've spent over nine years in technology, until recently I saw no point in moving to Silicon Valley.

Make Your Own Space

I am happy to be back. My stay in Silicon Valley is connected to my new career plans and does not involve a crazy pace. I am very busy but it's the first time I've been in the Valley for a longer time and I don't feel constantly under pressure. I am confident that my life goal and my professional goals are more coherent. My decision was preceded by years of experience when I learned how to manage my own psyche and run my business as an entrepreneur and—more importantly—how not to run it. To be able to function in Silicon Valley at ease you have to create your own space.

We Need a Definition for Creating Extraordinary Things

Many people while thinking of start-ups imagine nice offices, promo t-shirts, and free pizza. In reality a start-up is a test of a business model, a way of organizing work. Usually the job is exciting but stressful. Especially when we decide to move to Silicon Valley or generally to the United States. We start alone, without friends or family. It is a huge cost. You might think about why you do it.

Should people test themselves to create extraordinary things? I think so. However, we need a definition of what "creating extraordinary things" really means.

Some Specific Ideas, Definitions, Schemes

Many people come to Silicon Valley to get financing; this is kind of "financial tourism." Yet before we come here for money it is worth coming to one or two conferences to learn the local art of conversation. What's surprising in Silicon Valley is that everyone seems to know the financial jargon of fundraising. Taxi drivers and yoga teachers have no problem saying *company X has valuation Y, raises on SAFEs, without Cap, at a discount.* It is incredible!

It is actually not difficult to learn those terms. All it takes is reading a few books or some blogs. But if you come here without knowing them you might feel less competent. It is not true; of course, it is just a question of learning a few specific ideas, definitions, and schemes.

Crowd Thinking

The Valley is a place inhabited by wise, progressively thinking people who constantly question status quo and create new realities. On the other hand it is a closed "ecosystem," which means that many people have similar ideas on various subjects.

So in contradiction to the prevalent idea about the originality of this place you might easily fall prey to *crowd thinking* and start thinking exactly the same as everybody else. A part of tech environment and the local press lives on stereotypes and truisms that appear and become fashionable until a new trend comes up—something that before was unthinkable—and changes the paradigm. So it is worth knowing what *everybody is thinking* at a given time and ask if we think the same, and why. Recently Elon Musk introduced a new trend in the Valley—"thinking from the ground up," meaning questioning absolutely *everything*. I think it is good.

Technology with Capital "T"

There are start-ups that stand out on the sole merit of their technology. But it has to be technology with capital "T." Companies who just make another app and who want to make it big in the Valley, need to build a large network of contacts or have great sales people and an original sales strategy. So in this sense they resemble classical companies. Thus why is it worthwhile to be in the Valley? For sure if we have groundbreaking technology, something deserving a patent. The Valley is one of the few places in the world where it is easier to commercialize innovation. You should consider coming to the Valley if your technology is targeted at programmers or designers. If your target client is advertising, fashion, financial sector, or real estate the best place to operate is New York.

Therefore there is no clear answer if and when one should come to Silicon Valley. That depends on many factors. Sometimes it is not worth leaving where you are—some businesses can be built from any place on the globe.

Plans for the Future

Mature Questions...

Until recently I had no specific plans for the future. What I have done so far went like this: *We are a group of friends, we work together, it's cool.* And it was cool, up to a point. Now I understand better what I want to achieve. Maybe because I ask myself more mature and harder questions.

Positive Social Impact

At present I am building an investment fund based on positive social impact principle: so for the start-ups and tech companies that create positive changes in our world. Social good tech companies that interest me have a chance to enjoy great commercial success and, as a result, even more positively influence the environment. Although I believe in nonprofit organizations our fund focuses on for-profit companies. We want to prove that it is possible that you can have excellent return on investment, investing only in companies established to make something good in the world and not just make money. A good example of social good tech company is Tesla producing electric cars, which is good for the environment. In my opinion positive impact companies represent a new trend. Research shows that companies with such profile find it easier to employ the best workers, have easer time creating positive PR as journalists like to write about companies, which change the world for the better.

At the same time I am running a San Francisco based entrepreneur community impact.tech. I feel I have found my niche. My friends support me greatly. I am glad I am in my element.

How Can We Help Humanity?

Seth and I have been running Fifty Years together. We want to prove something, answer the question how we can really help humanity. It is not an easy task, we have a lot of work and the answers we'll be probably collecting over the next 50 years!

The role of investor is not limited to just financing. At Innovation Nest I learned how to work with entrepreneurs. Investors can be helpful also with their network of contacts and experience—they give advice on how entrepreneurs should best manage their time and be most effective. How to help entrepreneurs is a very interesting question for me. At present we have eight companies in our portfolio. They are all very impressive and deal with a variety of problems.

Supporting Socially Responsible Companies

Fifty Years fund is a long-haul adventure. I think I could work there till the end of my life. It's a long distance mission. The fund is still small. We plan about 30 investments. The goal is to prove that our investment idea works and we can get excellent return on this kind of investment. In the next years we want to use significant funds to support socially responsible start-ups as well as the companies that want to make a better world by commercializing scientific discoveries and educating about the advantages of new technologies.

"Fifty Years Hence"

Establishing the fund we were inspired by Winston Churchill's 1931 speech "Fifty Years Hence," in which he predicted, among other things, artificial intelligence. He talked about it before the creation of Enigma and Alan Turing's research.

As late as in the 1970s and 1980s many software engineers did not believe that artificial intelligence would be created which shows even more how visionary Churchill's address was.

Churchill also predicted creating protein in vitro. I am a vegan and I am very interested in ways to create animal protein outside a living organism. We've recently invested in a company that deals with exactly that.

Women in IT

Women in Silicon Valley?

It is a cliché, but career path for women is harder. Young women have to be careful as by accident they might end up as a "nice add-on" to a business: *We'll invite you to a panel, to a conference, to dinner.* It's just that those "invitations" don't lead anywhere. Many women coming to Silicon Valley do not realize they do not get equal treatment with men. Especially so, if we consider the business and technological competence. My self-esteem is strong enough so I don't take particular interest in what people think about me. Fortunately I have skills and experience that is impressive even in Silicon Valley. With my story I proved something. Yet before you prove that *something* it's relatively tough. It's not just male discrimination. Women also discriminate against women. Men who are starting up probably do not need to prove that much to others! Women in business have to give more. It will eventually change when the proportions get even.

Positive Reality Filter

I have a positive reality filter—if something did not work out today, it will work tomorrow. Maybe it is a filter that stops me from getting a realistic view of the world. Maybe that because of my gender I had come across many closed doors. I don't know that. I don't think something didn't work because I am a woman. I tend to think what to do better as an entrepreneur, investor, salesperson. If something doesn't work out I ask myself how I can find a different solution. Men also need to fight for their own! There are, by the way, many levels of discrimination, not just the gender ones. Being a "white European" I already am quite privileged in my life.

"Get Lost"

There are still many "old school" institutions and VC funds. When a young woman appears at a meeting like that, a male-female context occurs where competence is of no or little importance. I managed to survive this phenomenon. I never went to any "dinners." But you have to notice certain things, think and draw conclusions: *Aha, a dinner meeting has a different character than lunch or breakfast.* Sometimes the other party doesn't have any ill intentions. I don't have a simple advice about how to act in such unclear situations. When someone writes to me "let's meet for a drink" I respond that on principle I never meet after work. I can meet for breakfast or lunch. The message is simple: "Get lost!" You can create your own circle and go your own way without worrying if someone is now calculating your "chromosome configuration."

Ellen Pao

There has been a lot of commotion regarding Ellen Pao. Smarter men avoid ambiguous situations and subtexts. Still, some women decided to speak publicly of what's been going on. They showed great courage. They sacrificed a part of their lives and had to expose their privacy. Thanks to women like Ellen Pao we now know more about the problems of male-female relations at work. More women speak openly of *bro* culture, sexism, of what goes on at conferences, of pretty hostesses employed as "decorations." Talking about it creates certain norms.

I have a feeling the situation is slowly changing.

Bro Culture

Working in IT industry women often need to *downplay* their femininity. I have an impression that in Silicon Valley there are no dresses. It's just such dress code, and that's it. Myself, I never switched to jeans and t-shirts and I do wear dresses but I know women who changed. Tech women have a male lifestyle. I try to fight it but I still get surprised when I see someone with full make-up on. "A theoretical physicist doesn't wear dresses?" Oh, those stereotypes!

Pattern Recognition

The percentage of women taking technology courses is much smaller than men. Work in tech is hard. Regardless whether you are a programmer or not you have to know how to deal with tech co-founders and tech work-ers. Large start-ups carry large risks and women sometimes don't want to take that risk. I also know that in theory women have more trouble getting financing.

The work of an investor consists in "pattern recognition" and historically the most successes and "exits" in tech have been achieved by men. That's why investors more often invest in men. It is caused by selection bias. This tendency is slowly changing. Many investors try to invest in women to have diverse, male-female teams. A mixed team portfolio looks better and there is also research showing that the presence of women in management positions correlates with success.

There is a growing number of Silicon Valley start-ups that were co-founded by women. At present it is around 25 percent. In Europe, including Poland, the percentage is much lower. In comparison, in Brooklyn start-ups co-founded by women comprise around 40 percent of companies in that area. This is an amazing number but it is connected to the specific of the industry. In New York fashion industry is very developed and, as elsewhere in the world, many women are professionally involved in fashion tech.

Is it Harder for Women to Work in IT Environment?

I think so, but personally I have not experienced this. But my sister Basia who is a programmer and sociologist and deals with gender issues would have confirmed. I know there is a strong "male element" to my way of thinking. I tend not to identify myself just through my gender. This is why I don't feel gender discrimination even working in male environment.

Still, I think women have it harder. At the "Youth in Leadership" conference where I presented a paper many women asked me how I managed to break through the barriers, overcome the "glass ceiling," and become successful in a male world. They all said that working for corporations can be very hard and sexist comments are common.

Our Success or a Team Success?

Women often undervalue themselves and are not able to tell themselves *I did it! I achieved it!* They don't acknowledge their success. That's why they don't talk about it. Research shows that women more often attribute success to the whole team while men have a tendency to take personal credit for the team's work.

Judging by this example—everything that I achieved before was the effect of the work of a fantastic group of people. I always stress that. The whole team was responsible for our successes. Such results cannot be obtained by one person. Now, when I begin to walk alone I feel an enormous burden on my shoulders.

Meetups for Women

These meetings are important. Women want to share their observations, their history. Sheryl Sandberg in *Learn In...*[1] stresses how important it is to have role models. Meetups for women are called to show that among us there are women who are successful. Such events help us focus on the goal: *since this person did it, there is a chance I can do it too.* There are also many support groups in which participants share their experiences. Such activities stop further exclusion of women. That's why I think that in today's world and at the present stage of evolution women's organizations are necessary. And if women want to meet, they should!

Ending on a Personal Note

The Biggest Success

Hard to say.

I've always been proud of Applicake team and from the work culture that we managed to create. That was something very special for me and it still matters a lot to me.

When I think of what I'll be doing for the next few years I feel proud of the path I have chosen. Although I cannot yet justify this pride with any concrete achievements as we are just starting, but even if we are not successful I feel I am participating in something important.

---

[1] Sheryl Sandberg, *Learn in: Women, Work and the Way to Learn.*

Milestone

Milestones. Founding Applicake, decision to get involved in Base CRM, Y Combinator, Innovation Nest, Fifty Years.

I hope Fifty Years is my next one…

Sprinter or Marathon Runner?

In my life I follow the advice I got from my parents, particularly one simple principle that I recommend to all: "Treat people like you would like to be treated."

While the best business advice I ever got came probably from my friend Jerry Colonna—a mentor of many entrepreneurs and investors. He told me: "You need to know if you are a sprinter or a marathon runner." It means anyone of us can be successful. Some people will do great in the sprint category—they will build start-ups and for them it will be the right work environment. Other people are marathon runners who slowly build certain value and on that fundament they keep creating further.

And life is generally more like a marathon which means you don't have to optimize of what you want to do next year but rather you should think what you want to do for the rest of your life, trying not to get burned out on the way.

That was a good piece of advice for me. I am a marathon runner.

Leisure Time…

I dance, go to yoga, run. On weekends I try to take my mind off work.

I meditate. I recommend Headspace app. Fifteen minutes a day is enough and indeed you can train your brain to release control.

One thing I miss in San Francisco is art.

***

The interview took place on July 29, 2015 in San Francisco. Updated January 29, 2016.

CHAPTER 3

Wellfitting

Start-up as a Lifestyle

Sisters, understand each other without words.

Julia Krysztofiak-Szopa—with her sister Amelia established start-up Wellfitting. Earlier she was a director of California accelerator Blackbox. She is the mother of little Rysio.

She studied philosophy at the Warsaw University. Recipient of Erasmus program in Belgium. For three years she lived in Silicon Valley where she "switched" to the Californian mindset. She lived in Zurich. Presently she lives in Poland, CEO of Start-up Poland.

Passionate about artificial intelligence, design, and bras.

Amelia Krysztofiak—studied Mediterranean culture at the Warsaw University. Was part of Erasmus student exchange program at the University of Lisbon. Her stay in Portugal changed her life: she learned to overcome barriers in personal communication and learned to speak Portuguese. The people she met in Portugal are still the source of her business contacts.

Amelia worked as a receptionist, bra-fitter, developed the Polish section of Yelp, cooperated with Geek Girls Carrots. During several months of her stay in Silicon Valley with sister Julia established and developed Wellfitting start-up. She lives in Warsaw and works as a UX designer. Recently she also became a mom.

A trip to Silicon Valley is also important for young Europeans as Silicon Valley has no ethnic bias. Newly arriving Europeans usually have some dose of chauvinism, which they need to quickly discard, otherwise they will not get any support in Silicon Valley, neither social nor substantive.

Regardless where I am and what challenges I encounter I can be productive, getting lots of satisfaction from life and taking advantage of what the challenge brings.

—Julia Krysztofiak-Szopa

We are the each other's closest persons. We know each other well. We cooperate well. When I need assistance it is obvious that first I turn to my closest family.

—Amelia Krysztofiak

During our first interview Julia lived in Zurich and Amelia was there for a visit. The three of us talked on Skype.

I asked Julia to tell me about her experience working at Blackbox accelerator in Silicon Valley and also about the milestone in her life that was becoming a mom. Julia and Amelia told me also about running their start-up Wellfitting.

Julia: Balkonetka.pl

Lobby of the Well Endowed

My start-up adventure started with bras. I was looking for an Internet store where I could get my size brassiere. I have ample bosom and finding the right lingerie has always been a challenge. Finally, at gazeta.pl forum I found a women's community "Lobby of the well-endowed."[1] The group had about 200 participants sharing tips on where to shop for bras. It turned out the women from the "Lobby of the well-endowed" order bras in the UK.

First Polish Start-up—AdTaily

Intrigued by this situation I started a blog where I began describing my quest for bras. It was called Balkonetka.pl, which created a community of bra-geeks.

---

[1] (*Lobby biuściastych*—in Polish).

As the result of Balkonetka's success I got a job at the first Polish start-up AdTaily founded by Jakub Krzych and Marcin Ekiert. My job title was Community Manager partly because being a blogger myself I understood other bloggers' problems. AdTaily was selling advertising for blogs and small publishers.

I also worked for another start-up InFlavo—which at that time was a social media branch of Rafał Brzoska's Inpost company and remotely for California start-up GinzaMetrics.

Balkonetka.pl

In the meantime Balkonetka community was growing. I decided to develop the blog format and add additional functions. I started with creating a bra catalogue. I suggested that women post pictures of bras they got online and write comments. My husband programmed the back-end of the portal, I designed the front-end.

Balkonetks.pl was gaining popularity so Polish lingerie manufacturers who noticed Internet-based social networks in the segment of large size bras turned to me with questions. They asked to present their brand or review their products.

In 2010, I met Anna Matczak from Łódź, owner of COMEXIM lingerie company. She helped us a lot. She also sent us some bras for review.

I always treated Balkonetka as a hobby and it never became my source of income. Today Balkonetka is a popular forum with over 70,000 registered users.

Julia: California

Into the Unknown—Mountain View

In 2012, my husband got an offer from Google to work in Mountain View, in Silicon Valley. We decided to move to the United States. We made a quick decision, reversing our earlier plans. We left for Mountain View in October after having moved to our own apartment in Warsaw just a few months earlier, in mid-August. So we decided to give up settling down in Poland and explore the unknown in California.

Painful Reality Check

We started in Palo Alto, the heart of Silicon Valley. We were shocked by real estate prices and high cost of living. Even though everything was high quality but the price was awfully steep. Everyday expenses consumed the majority of our budget. It was a painful reality check.

Red Tape

Because of the visa restrictions I was not allowed to get a regular job in the United States. My decision from a few years ago not to finish my degree turned out to be problematic for the immigration authority since people with "no education" we had trouble with getting working visas and waiting for a green card takes years.

Julia: Blackbox Accelerator

A That Time Blackbox Was Still a Start-up

Thanks to many contacts provided by Piotr Wilam I ended up in Blackbox accelerator. The founder, Fadi Bishara, was looking for a person with whom he could start and run that enterprise. At that time Blackbox was still a start-up. Since I was looking forward to new challenges and wanted to build my network in a new environment I was happy to accept the proposal to join in. In 2012, I started as a volunteer at Blackbox accelerator. Initially there were just the two of us—Fadi Bishara and I. When a company has just two employees you have to do everything. This was our case.

Soon we were joined by a third person, Jenny Jung and within a few months we were able to start the first two-week educational-training program for start-ups from outside the United States. The goal was to prepare the start-ups for the first investment round in Silicon Valley.

Important Accelerator in Silicon Valley

At the time the headquarters of Blackbox was a mansion with swimming pool and a giant garden. Fadi's idea was to create an accelerator for international start-ups. Blackbox had a few guest rooms so acted as a hostel.

Program participants could live there, work and spend leisure time. We organized many meetings and events to which we invited celebrities of Silicon Valley.

I ran three accelerator programs. Those first two-week long programs established Blackbox's reputation as an important Silicon Valley accelerator.

To the best alumni Blackbox team offered long-term consulting and assistance in raising investment rounds and building a team in the United States.

"Think globally" —What Does It Mean?

Start-ups applying for Blackbox are in various stages of development. Some founders who just begin to develop their idea are convinced that their project will change the world—very often they think very highly of themselves.

We also cooperated with companies who were already operating on their local markets and sometimes got funding in their countries. We had such companies, among others, from Latvia and Argentina. Such founders who had investors back home and applying for financing in Silicon Valley had to figure out how to manage those investments. We had to work together to create strategies to enter new markets.

What all those start-ups had in common was the wish to put their products on the global market. For the early stage start-ups with just an idea it was important to think globally from the very beginning. The question was, what did it really mean?

Accelerator World

Many accelerators have been created in recent years all over the world, not just in the United States. Y Combinator is considered the most prestigious one in the world and many institutions dealing in incubation of young companies try to emulate it.

There are accelerators for young companies less than a year old. They can be admitted to such an accelerator only if they don't yet have an investor.

Some accelerators accept both advanced start-ups with investors as well as complete beginners. From the accelerator's point of view cooperation with the founder makes sense if the start-up is likely to increase its value in near future. Incubating institutions usually have shares in companies that they look after. Those shares become valuable only at the beginning of the investment round or at the exit, meaning the sale of the company. That's why accelerators will always work toward getting funding for the start-up.

Dominant Trends

Considering a start-up for their program, accelerators take into account several factors. Priority is for the start-ups who have a better chance of getting the financing round.

Investors, not just those in Silicon Valley, follow trends currently dominant on the market. If a key Valley investor has invested in a new technology it is likely that others will want to add this technology segment to their portfolio. For instance in our industry three most important "bra start-ups" got financing at roughly the same time. Later things cooled down and we don't hear of new start-ups at this particular market.

On the other hand, unfortunately, there is a catch. If investors take interest in a new segment as a fad and in the next few years the fad doesn't bring spectacular results another company in that segment will have a hard time to enter the market. Investors usually think in stereotypes and draw quick conclusions. That's why start-ups looking for financing should study the trends on the market of financial rounds. It is worthwhile to get on the trend bandwagon with the right idea.

Julia: Start-ups in Silicon Valley

Who Stays in America, Who Goes Back Home?

Most start-ups go back to their home countries. The decision to go back is a part of a strategy. We had an entrepreneur from Argentina who decided to expand into the whole Latin America. It is an enormous market and that decision was his global strategy. So although he got U.S. financing, he went back to Argentina. He now develops his product in South America and comes to Silicon Valley as needed.

Physical presence in the United States is not a necessity. You can think globally from any place in the world. Investors, of course, want to pour their resources into people who are present in the Valley. It they want to talk with a CEO from their portfolio company they prefer direct contact, not Skype. If a start-up begins to move in the wrong direction you need to ask the founder for explanation. After all when you put hundreds of thousand or even millions of dollars into somebody's pocket it is obvious you want to feel secure and be able to meet and talk.

Silicon Valley "Stamp"

Silicon Valley is a very good brand worldwide, especially in Poland. I learned that when I worked in Blackbox. I was inundated by e-mails and invitations to connect on LinkedIn or Facebook. Many people asked me for an introduction, assistance, support, and advice. I had never experienced such an avalanche of contact requests. I also was asked to write short articles. When I moved back to Europe my personal brand significantly decreased. I saw how unstable and short-lived is such "demand." When my signature no longer carries the "stamp" of Silicon Valley I am no longer attractive for the industry and people lose interest in me since they feel that knowing me or being in contact with me they can get ahead.

Within my means I always try to help but I was physically unable to answer every e-mail, request, or invitation. Where I could and believed my support would make sense I tried to lend a hand. It also felt good when I could offer advice.

Reform the Thinking Process

In Blackbox I cooperated with people from all over the world. Some European start-ups come to Silicon Valley convinced they know every-thing and they just need money to keep growing. Their want to act according to their internal plan and don't take any, even constructive feedback. Unfortunately such attitude of newbie European start-ups stands in negative contrast to the established Silicon Valley start-ups.

The success of newly arriving start-ups depends on whether they manage to reform their thinking process and accept assistance from people who think differently and are open to the world.

Success of the Seed Round

Many foreign start-ups define success as raising the seed fund. This misjudged approach to success has always shocked me. The goal of many start-ups coming to Silicon Valley is asking for money. And there is nothing wrong with it. The question is, if those start-ups actually have an idea how to grow. There are start-ups that ended their existence with getting funding and nothing more came out of it. Although it might happen at some point...

Facing Failure

Many times I witnessed a situation where start-up founders did not acknowledge reality and denied having made any mistakes. They try to put the blame on other co-founders and accuse them of misunderstanding the product and the chosen strategy. This is the model of denial combined with scapegoating. We've seen the denial mechanism among all start-uppers regardless of the country the come from or level of experience.

When we face failure we try to explain to ourselves and to others that it was not our failure. It is a very universal, human behavior.

More on Failure

We need to talk about failures, we need to help one another and share our experiences. In Silicon Valley failures are glorified, there is even a cult of failure. Some young people would like to experience a spectacular failure to tell stories about it later. We should now define what we mean by failure and what it means to avoid it at any cost. Young entrepreneurs in Europe fear failure more than their colleagues across the ocean that's why they often choose safe strategies and want to preempt negative consequences. In Silicon Valley, on the other hand, people think that if something doesn't work out, so much for that, they have to keep going.

For me failure is a breakup of a start-up or a project for personal reasons, for instance when the founders have a falling out. We do not have this problem, as we are sisters. I would be scared of such failure.

Polish Tech Competence

A giant advantage of Polish start-ups, which often lacks in those from Western Europe or North America is technological competence. In the United States, tech competence is often outsourced to teams in Asia or Eastern Europe. Start-ups from Poland and from Eastern Europe have excellent programmers so they don't need to look for them abroad and even if they do decide to outsource they can find people in the same country. It is a very competitive potential compared to the challenges facing start-ups in the United States. Programmers recruited in Silicon Valley compete in their salaries with programmers from such giants as Google, Facebook, or Apple which of course creates a great financial burden for start-ups.

Julia: On Start-ups

When Do You Start Thinking Globally?

From the very beginning. This is a more effective strategy than focusing on your own market with the goal of globalizing the product in the next phase of development. You have to remember, however, that the markets differ from one another. A product that sells well on the Polish market might not work on the German or American one. For instance in the United States, there are many applications that simplify the use of personal checks, as the checks are still a popular form of payment. In Poland or Germany practically no one uses them. That's why a check-reading product for your phone has no chance on those markets.

There are many ideas that work only for a particular market. This refers mostly to products related to insurance and Internet payments.

My advice would be to start thinking about the global market from the very beginning, when the idea gets born. In the next phase of operation you should adjust the product to particular demands of smaller markets. It is much easier to have great ambitions if you are thinking of yourself as a global start-up. And this is a natural way of thinking. If you think you are a Polish start-up that will soon become, or is becoming, a global hit this reflects smaller ambition.

As the Oarsmen in the Boat

It is important that team members are in synch. We waste a lot of time if we keep going over and over the same issues with various people in the group. The core team needs to share a common understanding of what they do, where they go, what are the company's values.

A good team works without much talk. It's kind of like oarsmen in a boat—they don't need to say things like: you need to use the left oar, while I use the right one. They just keep rowing.

Division of Competence

Another important feature of a successful team is dividing competence. It is dangerous when the founders' competences overlap.

In Blackbox, we organized meetings called *co-founder dinners*. Those were match-making events attended by founders looking for co-founders. The majority of participants were from the business side, only occasionally they represented the tech side. It means there is great demand for programmers, techy co-founders.

Leadership and the ability to engage people who will work for nothing or for long hours are very important characteristics of a leader. If a start-up wants to attract specialists with unique or rare skills it should look for ways to encourage those people to join in. That's why the founder should be charismatic, should be able to motivate and lead.

Start-up that lacks the division of competence, or strong leadership can, of course secure financing, as anyone can do that, but it has much less chance for long-term success.

In our team we never fought about division of competence. Our activities are coordinated and it is always clear what is Amelia's job, what is Julia's job.

What Makes Start-up Work Attractive

People who decide to work for start-ups want to have impact on what goes on in their work environment. They want to be able to independently determine the results of their work, take responsibility for their decisions, and feel that the result is entirely up to them.

People working for corporations, on the other hand, often feel comfortable being a cog in a larger machine. They prefer the shared responsibility of a team as in this way responsibility gets somewhat blurred. It puts their minds at ease.

What is attractive and unique in working for a start-up is the possibility of developing the product, of putting one's own ideas into practice. Start-ups don't have the typical organizational structure of large companies. There are no managers to whom you need to report. This is a most attractive element of start-up work.

The Myth of Working Around the Clock Is True

A harder element of a start-up job is work around the clock.

Work for a start-up goes on 24/7, 365 days a year and sometimes it is hard to find time for yourself. Many will not decide to establish their own start-up for this very reason. Many people in Silicon Valley have extreme work habits. We have friends who get up at 7 a.m., sit at their computer at 8 and get up at 2 a.m. They code nonstop and this is all they do. Sometimes they will go to an industry meetup. You hear about people with no personal life because they run a company. The myth of people working 20 hours a day is actually true.

Mental Hygiene

In spite of 20-hour workday the awareness of mental hygiene in Silicon Valley is very high. A popular way to recharge internally is meditation.

Neglecting mental hygiene can have negative impact, especially if our body is depleted—we can have trouble dealing with stressful situations and in building positive interpersonal relations. There is a whole spectrum of problems, which we tackle better if we are at peace with ourselves.

In Europe caring for mental hygiene is still considered "luxury" or means that we have psychological or psychiatric problems. Of course this keeps changing, although the number of meditating CEOs is much smaller in Europe than in California.

In the United States, people use many mobile applications that help meditate. I think that investing in mental hygiene is one of the many factors that make the Bay Area stand out compared to many other places in the world.

Julia: On Inspiration and Science

Inspiration?

When I started working at Blackbox accelerator I was impressed by people who arrived there. They inspired me greatly.

I was inspired by those who were not scared to admit that they did not know something, that something didn't work out, that they struggled, that they were sensitive. They were very successful but they also reached out for help to others.

I was inspired by entrepreneurs who came to Silicon Valley with their novel ideas, with their minds open to the world, with the expectation to go an extra mile to achieve the most.

I Learned Not To Be Afraid

My stay in Silicon Valley changed me a lot. I became open to others, to not knowing things, to asking for help and—last but not least—I learned not to fear. Not to fear that someone would hurt me, judge me. I learned not to be afraid to trust people.

Before coming to California I was very distrustful with overblown ambitions and wanted to be better at everything.

American Dream…

Taking into account all the limitations, in my opinion I used my time in California very effectively.

My work at Blackbox accelerator and the decision to have a child had perfect timing and fueled my development. The contacts I made at Blackbox are with me even today; I learned a ton of things and got greatly inspired. I don't regret one moment of that stay, although it was a tough experience, especially when it turned out our "American dream" was not exactly what we imagined…

Relationships with Entrepreneurs Are Knowledge

Building relations with successful entrepreneurs is an energizing and important element in the process of creating a start-up. I was greatly inspired by Marcin Treder. We need to build relations with all kinds of businessmen, with people who are active, not just with start-up founders. You should also know the operating mode of a "traditional" business. We learned a lot from Ms. Anna Matczak, who's been running textile companies for many years. Her advice and intuitions work also in tech business. You have to learn from all people with experience.

In Poland it is difficult to find companies where family traditions were passed from generation to generation. It is harder to learn from role models that are simply not present in Poland. So to establish business relations you need to travel to more advanced "ecosystems."

Open Up to Others

The phenomenon of Silicon Valley consists in having access to people from whom you can learn. For people coming from Poland this is an amazing experience. At any gathering you can meet leaders of the greatest technological companies.

In Silicon Valley there is no mental–financial barrier. People who are today very rich and are entrepreneurs or investors 20 years ago were the same as us—they were building their start-up. Being open to others is the foundation of today's Silicon Valley.

How Silicon Valley Stands Out

First—the sunshine… The weather is among the key elements why people in California are so optimistic and friendly toward others.

In California everyone wants to be helpful. In Poland, while working with start-ups, I often encounter this attitude: *I have an idea but I will not tell you, as it is a secret.* This is very European thinking. I experienced this kind of mentality also in Switzerland. Many people in the start-up community will not tell you what they work on, as they are scared someone will steal their idea.

Meanwhile it is not the idea that counts but its execution. To realize an idea is the key to success. In Silicon Valley everyone talks about their ideas.

Spreading the Pool of Goodness in the World

Many people in Silicon Valley are newcomers and typical self-made men who have already achieved a lot and put the bar high. Comparing Silicon Valley to Switzerland you can see the difference in priorities among people with thick wallets. European industry private equity investors' meetings have the subtext of *How to grow and protect your wealth*, since they are mostly interested in "increasing their riches." In Silicon Valley the main motivation is different—investors want to learn how to use their money to make the world a better place, how to form the next generation of investors and entrepreneurs, how to make VC industry assist innovation more effectively. The business community in Silicon Valley is interested in spreading the pool of goodness in the world with the available funds, while entrepreneurs in Switzerland (and the rest of Europe) are interested in growing their private bank accounts.

People who join Silicon Valley community must learn to respect the "Valley values" and culture of openness. When a visiting investor from Europe says he is mainly interested in *growing and protecting his wealth* no one in Silicon Valley will treat him seriously.

Historical Background

European societies have evolved from a class and feudal system. There were peasants and feudal lords, powerful aristocratic families, and royal dynasties. Interclass migration was practically impossible. A peasant woman could not become a duchess. It would never happen.

And since feudalism has been gone for a few centuries, fiefdoms and serfdom no longer exist, European societies are still weary of cross-class migration, especially of the upward mobility from the poorer to the richer strata. It is especially striking in the affluent European states. In Poland this phenomenon is not so obvious since 50 years of Communist rule destroyed class divisions. Yet in countries like Switzerland you have upper and lower class neighborhoods where upward migration is impossible or very difficult.

In the United States, cross-class migration is also difficult but there is permission to dream about it. This lacks in Europe. In Poland a grotesque symbol of breaking into the upper class is the character of Nikodem Dyzma.[2]

The United States is a country of immigrants. In the 19th century when someone came to America being even a descendant of someone "important" in Europe, in the New World his background was irrelevant. What mattered were the "primal skills" and the ability to manage in new and difficult circumstances.

My Advice for Newcomers to Silicon Valley

First of all, you have to open your mind. You should not come to Silicon Valley just to raise money. You come here for mental transformation. Don't be afraid to aim high. Sometimes we avoid being too ambitious because small ambitions seem to have a better chance of success than the large ones. With big ambitions it is easier to fail. But you should not be scared to fail. Failures are temporary.

I would also recommend having realistic expectations about coming to Silicon Valley. I met many Polish start-ups that came to the Valley convinced that within two weeks they would raise money. They have read things, heard stories... Young start-uppers seem to think that raising a

---

[2] *Kariera Nikodema Dyzmy (The Career of Nikodemus Dyzma)* by T. Dołęga-Mostowicz. The novel might have inspired Jerzy Kosinski's *Being There*. [translator's note].

financial round in Silicon Valley takes just a few days since the legal system favors entrepreneurship and investors make their decisions quickly. Sometimes you can get funding in a short period of time. We know of such cases. However, Silicon Valley investing community and ecosystem is a self-regulating mechanism. What matters is trust, reputation, and track record.

People who come to Silicon Valley and are completely unknown, don't have any business relationships will not be able to raise the investment round within two weeks.

That's why my advice to the young Polish start-uppers is to be open to others and start building long-term relations, not always focused on direct profit. You should build relationships that will prove rewarding in due time.

What Are the Prerequisites for a Start-up Coming to Silicon Valley?

None. You can, or even should, come to Silicon Valley with an idea and take advantage of your stay. You can also come when you have an established position on your local market. There are absolutely no stiff rules.

Julia: Globally and Locally

They Begin to Think Globally

Even if a start-up comes to California planning to get financing but is not successful it leaves Silicon Valley enriched with priceless experience. The mental transformation is essential since these people begin to think globally.

American start-ups automatically start at the global market since the whole world speaks English. Even if initially they offer their services just on the American market people in other countries will be able to access those services. This is what usually happens.

Meanwhile when a start-up offers services on the Polish market the chance that someone outside of Poland will be able to use that service is very slim.

That's why opening to the global market and understanding that the market is within arm's reach is the greatest value that practically everyone takes home from Silicon Valley.

The Polish Complex

Another key issue concerns self-esteem. Successful Silicon Valley entrepreneurs who first raise the seed round and then A, B, and C rounds, whose start-ups are no longer start-ups and begin employing hundreds of people are, in essence, no different from us.

In Poland, on the other hand, and in other post-Communist countries we tend to think of ourselves as of "village poor." Our self-esteem is low. Polish start-uppers introducing their products to the American market often asked me questions coming from our Polish mentality steeped in inferiority complex.

They asked me if on their website they should say that the start-up came from Poland. Should they give their surname, or only given name in the e-mail address since the surname sounds Polish and the Americans will have trouble pronouncing it.

To be clear: yes, they should write they are from Poland! Yes, they should put their Polish-sounding name in the e-mail address.

Such questions and the fear of being associated with Poland come from our national complexes.

There are many foreigners in Silicon Valley whose names are difficult to pronounce and write but those foreigners are not afraid to be ostracized for not being called John Smith.

At the same time we, Poles, are often afraid or even ashamed of who we are and where we come from. We fear that we will get a "Polish stamp" and it will weaken our brand and image.

European Prejudices

In Silicon Valley no one cares if we are from Poland or some other place in the world. Our origin does not determine whether we will be successful or not. No one looks at us differently because we came from Poland. Feeling and realizing that we, Poles, do not stand out in any negative way helps Polish start-ups in Silicon Valley a lot.

Leaving for Silicon Valley is important for young Europeans also because there are no ethnic prejudices here. And sometimes newly arrived Europeans display a great dose of chauvinism that they need to discard, otherwise they will not find any support in the Valley, neither in substance nor socially.

What Matters Are the Merits of Enterprise

In Poland we have a tendency to judge people. When we talk about our project we are met with doubt, ridicule, negation. Young Poles coming to Silicon Valley are often afraid their idea or project will be laughed at.

In Silicon Valley no one will laugh at even the most niche project. Investors might decide that they are not interested in that segment or that they are not interested in a certain market or they might say they invest from five million upwards. In Silicon Valley what matters is the merit of the enterprise. In Poland blind criticism overshadows essential discussion.

Who Is to Blame?

Silicon Valley has a culture of action and optimistic outlook.

In Poland we are versed in the culture of complaint, we look for problems, obstacles, and the guilty party. In Poland there always is someone to blame. The law is to blame because it does not support enterprise; we blame a bad employee, low salaries, high taxes... It goes on and on.

At the same time we mythologize the West. Because in the West it is "different and better"...

Our Polish Generation Gap

In the United States, we met many Americans who say: "I have a start-up but you should see my dad's company! And my great-grandfather had the first department store in town..."

How many young people in Poland can say: "You should have seen my dad's company! And my great-grandfather..."

For the last 50 years there was no private business in Poland. Our generation gap comes from the fact that we have a whole generation of people who don't have any model of entrepreneurship whatsoever in their surroundings. Sometimes the only model of "enterprise" was an uncle growing flowers or an aunt trading sheepskin coats from Turkey…

Our mom in the early 1990s would drive her minuscule Fiat 126 to a fair in Bielsko-Biała and sell cheap tchotchkes. This is the kind of business tradition people of my generation had. Of course there was a small group of people who were businessmen but it was not common. In our circle of friends no one comes from a family of entrepreneurs.

Basic Financial Security

For the majority of young people in Poland the priority is finding a steady job to get basic financial security. There's nothing unusual about it. I remember well the time when my husband and I started working and make money. Such situation brings psychological calm, takes the burden off the shoulders. I remember the moment when financial insecurity disappeared.

Meanwhile living with constant uncertainty, wondering if we will be able to pay off the car loan, afford the kid's school tuition makes it hard for us to think about other, bigger things. That's why among young generation very few think of starting their own business or start-up. Although it has been slowly changing.

Julia: On Private and Professional Decisions

Decisions

In 2013, we decided to expand our family and have a baby. I also decided to start my own company.

A Bra that Fits

While in the United States, I kept my interest in the lingerie industry, especially in bras for women with large breasts. I discovered that in American Internet, in the segment of nonstandard sizes brassieres, the situation was similar to that in Poland five years earlier. Women were creating communities and placed group orders for bras. To my surprise I found out that women in America ordered bras from Poland. In the United States, it is practically impossible to get extra large size bras, so the women from the "bra community" use Google Translate to buy bras at COMEXIM company in Łódź or from the studio of Ewa Michalak, also in Łódź.

At Reddit.com the most active community of bra geeks is called "A bra that fits."

Wellfitting

I know the Łódź textile industry very well. I decided to consolidate my knowledge with the niche existing on the American market and connect Polish bra-lingerie manufacturing with the American demand. This is how the idea for Wellfitting originated.

We started Wellfitting with my sister a month before the birth of little Ryszard Jr.

Amelia: About Wellfitting

Bootstrapping

Initially Wellfitting was going to be the American version of Balkonetka. pl. We wanted to create an influential bra forum for American and global clients. However, we were not able to quickly program the whole application ourselves and we would need to pay someone for the complete project. When Wellfitting took off, the company account was at 200 dollars. We did not have larger capital. To get money we decided to bootstrap selling bras from Poland to the United States. It turned out to be a good idea. The bras began to sell.

Financing?

Why didn't we apply for financing? Maybe the stereotype about women was at fault. I was afraid that the investors would be more interested in our numbers and how the sales were growing rather than in our start-up.

In addition to that we had a baby on board, which consists a certain limitation. We would not have been able to show investor any aggressive growth of the company. We treated Ryszard Jr. very seriously; after all he was our "youngest board member."

We also had doubts about our ability to invest and well spend those hundreds of thousands of dollars from financing. We both dislike waste. We did not want to squander money. This way of thinking is certainly very limiting. Still, at this point we cannot tell if our course of action is right or not. For now we are happy with how Wellfitting is performing.

For Julia the fact that we did not decide on financial backing from the very start is a kind of personal failure but for me starting a business with your own means, without any outside money was a no-brainer.

Idealism

In Wellfitting we want to give choices to women who so far have none. Maybe we are idealists and we are idealistic about our mission.

But it is true that the offer of standard chain stores for women with extra-large breasts is very limited. In regular stores bra sizes end at size D or DD.

In Wellfitting we offer cup sizes all the way to R. Our chest sizes are 26 to 44 inches, compared to Victoria's Secret they start at 32 and end at 40.

Wellfitting is also for girls who are very slim. Among our clients there are many women with Asian names and Asian women often have slender build. They write us thank-you notes saying we are a godsend since for years they could not find the right bra.

Forty percent of our clients return and the number is growing. We have clients from North America, Australia, China, Korea, and Europe, mainly Spain, Sweden, and the UK.

American Clients

In the United States, the structure of our sales is very specific. Many of our clients live in little towns, mostly in the middle states. We also have clients in big cities, quite a few in California.

A large contingent of women needs to buy online as there is no lingerie store in their area.

Unlimited Exchanges

All our orders are shipped from Poland. We don't have a warehouse since every product is custom made. We fulfill basically every product wish of our clients. At the same time we offer a hundred days for return or exchange and unlimited number of exchanges which somewhat slims down our income but brings more returning clients. If a girl exchanges her bra a few times she will most likely stay with us.

At present our greatest challenge is developing a product that women will want to keep buying over many years. We want to create a new product and we are going to invest in it.

Competition

We face strong competition. But it motivates us! Our ambition is to raise the self-esteem of women who have larger breasts or larger/smaller body. We want women to always feel good about their bodies. In Wellfitting we don't just sell bras—we also sell self-confidence.

And although we have a competitive advantage of a wider range of bra sizes in this industry we are competing with all stores with lingerie sections. The clients of Victoria's Secret will not get a bra in 32K size so they will buy something smaller or larger. The fit will not be comfortable, but it will have to do. Our mission is showing women that there is an alternative for the mass market.

A $200 Bra

While in the United States, I decided to conduct an experiment—I went to various lingerie stores and asked to have a bra fitted for me. I went to large department stores and boutiques. Unfortunately, I could not find anything that worked. I could either get an ill-fitting bra or a bra that was incredibly expensive. In Palo Alto there is a store importing French and German lingerie; among others they carry Triumph, a brand that is popular in Poland. In that store the assistant fitted me the right bra but I would need to pay almost $200 for it!

Competing Bra Start-ups

In recent years three bra start-ups appeared on the market: "Third Love" and "True & Co" from San Francisco, both of which received funding in the Bay Area, and Israeli start-up "Brayola" which got financing in New York.

Initially the technology used by "Third Love" was very modern—there was a mobile application that let you anonymously measure your bra size. Today "Third Love" is a standard Internet store offering limited sizes, styles, and patterns.

There are also Internet boutiques selling specialized lingerie lines. We are also competing with eBay and Amazon.

Our Measure of Success

Our measure of success is the number of returning clients and their loyalty.

Lingerie brands are often segmented and attached to women's age. Victoria's Secret is targeting women that are younger and in their 30s. For mature women there are specialized luxury brands and no-name brands sold in chain stores. There is no brand name lingerie market for older persons.

Our ambition is serving women in all stages of life.

On Beauty Standards

The female image used by clothing brands is extreme and unrealistic. Women have to conform to certain standards of beauty, looks, and age. Fashion companies do not want to represent women in their 50s, sometimes even forties. And what about women in their 70s? Is there a fashion company representing an older generation? There are no 70-year-old models.

We would like our brand to serve women of various ages—from the moment when a young girl buys her first bra to the time when being a mature woman, maybe even retired, she wants to feel comfortable and at the same time look good, not necessarily sexy but elegant and luxurious.

Maybe we will grow old with our company and maybe we will keep modeling for it.

Two Actual Persons

I was the first Wellfitting model. Our newest lines we model together. Some people accuse us of wanting to show "tits on the Internet." We are personally involved in our company and I have an impression that it helps our communication with the clients. When our clients talk to us, when they write about us on Internet forums, share their observations, give feedback or criticize us they criticize two actual persons—Julia and Amelia. There is no feeling of anonymity in Wellfitting.

Our dream is building a strong client community around Wellfitting. We would like to involve them in promotions and let them become our models.

Julia: On Breakthrough Moments

A Breakthrough Moment: A Bra Fitting Party

When I lived in California I organized a bra fitting party in a friend's garden in Palo Alto. We invited several women aged 40 to 50. To create and easy mood we started with a glass of champagne and appetizers. Then I made a short presentation of our bras. I explained why it was important to have a well-fitting bra and we talked about places we bought our lingerie.

In the upstairs room I prepared a few dozens of bras in various sizes and styles. The participants could ask my advice I also helped them to choose the right bra. Then every lady could place an order for the chosen product.

After the party I received a lot of positive comments on Facebook and thank-you e-mails. I realized then that the women who came to the party were anonymous clients of no-name mass brands and our mission and Wellfitting mission is to serve those women, our clients, all their life.

Social Support Network

During the bra fitting party women asked me how they could become consultants and sell lingerie at similar events.

I realized then I had a product that was ideally suited to direct sale during intimate parties in people's private homes. Personal contact with a trusted person who can offer advice, hand in the product, and make the client at ease is very important. Personalized and well-planned direct sale is one of the avenues we want to pursue in Wellfitting. We want to build confidence and create a network of social support.

Professional Fulfillment

Personal success is made of balancing a happy family life and professional fulfillment. By professional fulfillment I mean working a job that I like, that I am good at, that makes me feel that I am making the world a better place that I make someone's life easier, while at the same time earning a living. This is my simplified definition of self-realization. The material aspect is the least important. If we fulfill the key conditions—meaning we do something well and it really has a positive impact on other people's lives, the money will follow.

Every Day Is a Success

My personal as well as professional success it the market debut of our first product.

We were able to put the first product on the market within two months of starting the company. The two of us were the only employees. We started from scratch. Amelia came to California in July and on September 21 I gave birth to my son. In such a short time, between Amelia's arrival and the child's birth we started a company and created the first product.

This is the success I'm really proud off. Is this my greatest success, I don't know. I think, in a way, every day is a success.

My Life Success

My next individual success is the ability to adapt to various conditions. It is not a success tied to a specific event. It is my life success.

Regardless of where I am and what circumstances I encounter I can function well drawing great satisfaction from life and taking advantage of what those circumstances bring.

You Should Blossom Where You've Been Planted...

Why we are in Zurich? It's a pragmatic story.

As young parents we wanted to raise the standard of living of our family. In Silicon Valley we could not afford it, especially, since we depended only on my husband's income. We decided to move back to Europe and Google offered my husband a position in Zurich.

This is the whole story.

It turned out that Zurich had many financial advantages—first of all the salaries are high and the taxes are low; real estate is not expensive, especially compared to rental prices in Silicon Valley.

All my life I cherished the notion that "you should blossom where you've been planted." This time I also followed that motto. After all our start-up is global and can be run from any place on Earth.

For Amelia our decision to come back to Europe was a critical moment. We were supposed to raise financing and suddenly it turned out we were not staying in Silicon Valley and leaving for Zurich.

A Family Company

In California we employ a representative responsible for logistics and sales. In Warsaw it is our mom that helps with the shipping—we are a family firm. In addition to the fact that as a family we understand each other perfectly—and mutual understanding is critical for start-ups—we also have complementary skills.

Amelia is a designer. She deals with logistics and products. She supervises shipping. She is in charge of customer support. She is in contact with the COMEXIM manufacturer. She also designs the website.

My field is marketing, developing company strategy, and sometimes coding for our website.

My Work as a Lifestyle

After coming to Zurich I wanted to better connect with the local community so I started working part time for a start-up developing financial technologies for private equity firms. My salary covers the daycare cost for my son. Since I don't have to take care of my son all day long I am less tired in the evening. Daycare is a great solution and make mothers' lives easier. When I get my second child I will also send him or her to daycare maybe even earlier than Richard Jr. I was very tired by the world of diapers and being confined to the four walls. Now, after coming home I take care of my child. When my son goes to sleep I work for Wellfitting.

Our start-up is my lifestyle. Had I devoted 50 hours a week to it the firm might be growing faster but in my current situation I work as much as I can. And I feel good about it.

Our Own Reality

We are definitely courageous and we are not afraid of other people's opinions. In this way we might be functioning in our own reality.

Develop Your Start-up Where Life Sent You...

My lifestyle was developed in particular circumstances, by the need to cope with the fact that I live here and I want to take best advantage of it. Moves are always stressful. You need to find an apartment, get organized. Beginning with the hardest things and ending with the everyday concerns—where will I live, how to commute to work?

When my husband and lived in Belgium for one-year during the Erasmus program it was easy. When we came to the United States, what we discovered on arrival was completely different from our expectations. It was incredibly stressful. Particularly the astronomical cost of living and the obstacles in obtaining working visas...

The Future?

Geographically I see myself in the United States. Mainly because I would like to be closer to the American client. I don't want to move to America for good but I would like to be there a few months a year.

Julia and Amelia: Women in IT World

Self-Promotion

Nature made it so that women have a lot more duties connected with motherhood. Many women are just tired, they don't have the energy and the drive to combine their role as a mother with a career.

Before becoming a mom I had lots of time for self-promotion. Today it is the last item on my to-do list. I just don't have time. But when you look at the demographics of start-ups I dare say that the most people in this group have not yet started a family and don't have kids. In this situation saying that women don't have time for promoting themselves seems illogical. Although of course not all women are into self-promotion.

Not a Single Application

When we started with the first edition of the educational program at Blackbox all application we received came from men. There was not a single female candidate.

Thanks to our efforts we managed to attract two women founders one from Denmark and a Polish woman living in the UK. They both received our scholarships and decided to come to the Valley and participate in the program. But we had to show great determination in finding women who would like to come to California.

During later editions we were getting gradually more and more applications from female founders but usually there were just a few for every group.

Females Only

Recently Blackbox started a separate program *females only*: Blackbox Connect for female founders. In each edition several female leaders take part. It means that finally they managed to reach out to women and get them interested in the acceleration program, although initially it was really hard. Less women in the start-up community is also due to the fact that generally women like to play it save. You can tell by the way we both act and how we run Wellfitting—an excellent example of how women avoid a gamble.

Surplus of Demand over Supply

In the Silicon Valley start-up ecosystem the gender parity is very unbalanced. You might bluntly say that there is excessive demand and limited supply. Men who come from abroad, risking their careers and giving up their earlier life usually look for a partner or a way to deal with their libido. In social situations it shows as a primal need. I am not judging it. I don't want to judge what is good and what is bad. This is just the way things are. I wouldn't say women have a harder time with this. It is a known fact that men are more active in picking up women than the other way round. At the same time men are more aggressive in their behavior while trying to win a partner than women trying to attract a guy. That's why women more often encounter unwanted advances especially in situations in which flirting or picking up is out of place. This distance should be controlled. For many women such situations are awkward and embarrassing.

I Have Never Been Patronized

IT industry in Silicon Valley is famous for mobbing females or even for sexual harassment and discrimination. Recently there was a notorious case of Ellen Pao. Women working in IT in the Valley are often not treated on a par with men, although personally none of us have been ever patronized.

When we were starting with Wellfitting we did get some humorous remarks or cynical smiles. But such situations happen to everyone. Many ideas bring out negative emotions. I would not blame our femininity for that.

"An Older Brother"

I've been married for many years. During both private and professional meetings where I am with my husband Ryszard men are less likely to "shorten the distance" and in a way they treat me with greater respect.

Apparently it is harder for women in Silicon Valley to get financing. Maybe this is a good idea to take along a man when you go to meet investors—a "pretend" older brother or husband to avoid awkward remarks from the gentlemen present and to be treated more seriously.

Amelia: Meetups for Women

Events addressed to women and organized by woman are becoming very popular and frequent. Such meetings usually get a lot of coverage in the media. This makes it easier to reach women who for various reasons are afraid to enter this community, traditionally perceived as masculine. This way even women who otherwise would not think of being a part of women environment get a chance to join in. For instance thanks to Geek Girl Carrots, for which I was a co-organizer, many girls begin to act with more confidence and learn to create professional connection on social platform. I know girls who started as participants and now organize Greek Girls Carrots events. They started coming to meetings because those gathering were created specifically for women.

Women-only meetings sometimes act as a springboard in the training of interpersonal skills. The meetings help women feel more at ease, more confident so that later they can function in mixed environment without unnecessary shyness.

Most Chores Fall on Women

In today's world pro-female actions have become trendy. As a result they oftentimes isolate, at least in theory and language, one gender from another.

What I find funny in those campaigns is the fact that from the career and development point of view the difference between men and women are not due to mentality or IQ level but the fact that only women can bear children, something that no man, no matter how he tries, is able to do.

When a child gets born most chores fall on women. One might even say that 99 percent of duties rest on women. Especially in the first months of a baby's life.

Just Being a Woman Doesn't Change Much

Why do we keep stressing that we women in the IT world, in technologies, in entrepreneurship have it harder? Since we completely overlook the difference between the sexes.

We often fail to notice that mothers or generally parents—have it harder than non-parents. There are fathers who are also very much involved in raising children. For those fathers it is also much harder to build a start-up than for someone with no kids.

That division of difficulty does not go along male–female line but along the families and childless couples or people with family responsibilities and those without. The mere fact of being a woman and having breasts and other female secondary sex characteristics doesn't change much, in my opinion.

Work or Kid?

When I gave birth the child took over the majority of my time and attention. At the same time there wasn't a day that I would not think of Wellfitting. I wanted that project to continue, I did not want to abandon it or forget about it. My involvement in the company is extremely important for me.

Such situation might apply equally to women and men.

However, if someone doesn't like their job or just puts up with it from nine to five and looks forward to the moment when they leave the office then regardless if it is a man or a woman they will always look forward to long vacations.

In Poland a paid maternal leave can last even a year. In the United States, there is no guaranteed maternal leave. Only some modern companies have introduced it—Facebook offers four months for both mothers and fathers. In Google a paid maternal leave lasts from 18 to 22 weeks. In Apple—18 weeks, including four weeks before giving birth.

My husband got eight weeks of paternal leave. During that time he took great care of the baby and was very excited about his new role. At the same time he always checked the company mail because he wanted to know what was going on in the team.

This shows the difference between people who are greatly involved in their work and those that treat it just as a coerced financial necessity.

That's why my life goal is doing the work that I love and not just what I have to do.

"I am Sorry but I Do Not Have Kids"

One day I was taking part in a women's meeting in San Francisco. The discussion focused on the popular Silicon Valley subjects of difficulties facing female entrepreneurs. There was also talk about how hard it is for women to get financing.

It was a few weeks after I had my baby. During the panel discussion I asked if the participants had any advice for a young mom-entrepreneur. I asked how to reconcile new reality that I was experiencing with the lifestyle of an entrepreneur.

There were five women on the panel and each of them answered: "I am sorry but I do not have kids." None of them could give me the answer to that, apparently simple question. I found it very amusing at the time. They were all mature women in their forties—not students entering adult life. They were women who consciously chose not to have a family.

We Are Getting Ourselves a Ball and Chain...

The mistake that we women often make is to take on too many duties. We feel responsible for the family and don't expect support from our partners. I mean psychological support and shared responsibility for what goes on in our home, for our child. For who takes the kids to preschool and who picks them up, who will stay home when they are sick. We women automatically become primary caregivers. We are raised like that; we've been trained for this. We tie a ball and chain to our leg and the ball slows us down in our everyday life. I can see it in my own life. I take on too many duties. It slows me down in other areas. It should change. You should get your partner involved in pulling that ball. It should be tied to two legs. It will be easier to pull.

My advice is that women should not be scared to be labeled as bad mothers for whom the career is more important than the child. They should not be afraid to shed some duties and delegate the responsibilities to their partners, who are, by the way, also parents.

Multitasking

It seems to me that women are more productive. You can see that especially in positions that require multitasking. It is difficult to multitask as a backhoe operator or working another typically male job.

In managerial and office positions, though, where you have to control many variables and where you interact on many levels—there, compared to men, women are more productive and effective.

Men can be more assertive and can say "no" or "I don't know." Women are in the habit of offering assistance. I have such a habit: "Of course, I can help you." If I know how, I always help.

"I am Awesome and My Ideas Will Change the World"

What are the differences between women in Silicon Valley and in Poland?

Before coming to the United States I went to many conferences or start-up meetings devoted to women's entrepreneurship. My feeling is that women running their own companies in the United States are much more assertive than women in Poland.

When I was meeting female entrepreneurs from 500 Start-ups or from Y Combinator or even women not necessarily directly involved in the start-up world they always struck me as very domineering, loud, projecting with diaphragmatic, trained voice, certain of their arguments and thinking that whatever they did was awesome and would change the world.

Women in Poland lack self-confidence and trust their abilities. Polish men, on the other hand, often feel that what they do is terrific and the best.

My Advice—Make the Logo Yourself!

I advocate self-study—teaching yourself what you need at a given time. My advice is not to become dependent on people with skills that we lack. In today's world where you have so much educational resource available for free or at small cost becoming dependent on someone for finances or skills is a trap.

To women who plan to found their business but are afraid that they don't know how to code, make graphic design, or create a logo, I suggest that they learn to code or design the logo themselves! Try creating something yourself. Only if you need an advanced product begin to look for help. We are able to learn many things ourselves, especially in the early stages of our business.

The Most Important Piece of Advice

Julia

This is not advice but more of a motto that you should follow:

There are always bumps on the road but you can always manage to get through them.

I always try to remember that, even if I keep failing at something. Everything is temporary, not just failures, also successes and you just have to learn to cope with that.

Amelia

The piece of advice is short and I don't remember who gave it to me.

Trust your gut feeling.

Short. Common sense. Helps making decisions.

The Interview Took Place on June 22 and 24, 2015.

I met again with Julia and Amelia in San Francisco in mid-November.

The girls had an interview for Y Combinator on Saturday November 14, 2015. Just being invited to an interview is a great achievement and testifies to the quality of the product and a novel strategy of a start-up. Although this time Wellfitting didn't get a spot at the most prestigious accelerator in the world, Julia and Amelia are very happy about the interview. I asked them to tell me how the conversation with Y Combinator went and how they had prepared for it.

Interview

It was our second tryout. For the first time we applied to Y Combinator last year. But then we didn't even get an interview. This time we got invited and the conversation went very well. It was a fast exchange: question—answer, like ping-pong. At the end of the day we already knew the answer. All applicants get the answer the same day.

Although the reply was negative we got very valuable feedback—Y Combinator got our idea. We also found out that we have a good team. Our weak suit is the suggested model of sale and distribution.

Accelerators try to optimize every edition of their programs so that after three months, at the end of the program, you can show gigantic growth of every participating start-up. And during Demo Day it is expected that the founders will get financing.

During the interview we were not able to convince Y Combinator that within three months we would be able to achieve the growth rate that would be attractive to investors. Maybe our strategy is still not scaled. We have to invent a better "growth mechanism," prove that our concept works and in the summer we'll be back to YC!

That was our experience with Y Combinator. Although we didn't get in it was a very instructive experience.

Preparations

We spent three days preparing.

We re-checked all the financial records of the company—we had a cheat-sheet with numbers regarding our business and the market. We wanted to feel confident during the interview.

We also had talks with people who had done interviews for Y Combinator. We received pointers from, among others, Jakub Krzych, Kate Scisel, or Fadi Bishara. They prepped us at a mock interview.

We Are Motivated by a Great Vision

If in the next months we improve our financial results then in the summer we will reapply.

In Wellfitting we have a broad vision. We want our message to reach the widest target group. We want women to believe in themselves and their self-worth. Our mission is not just selling bras—we could settle at selling just five hundred bras a month and it would be enough to make a living. But we are more ambitious than that. We want to change the stereotypes involved in women's perception of their bodies. We want to change it not just in Poland, not just in Silicon Valley but all over the world. We want to create a movement of powerful women who believe in themselves. This is our global start-up vision that we follow and that is our hallmark.

Wellfitters

In recent months we clarified our vision of distribution. We sell mostly via Internet and this kind of sale model works. Yet it is not fully scalable.

We absorb quite high costs of returns, exchanges, and customer service. Getting ready for the interview with Y Combinator we invented another, additional system of selling our products. In a way it resembles the system of Avon. We calculated how many consultants (Wellfitters) we would have to recruit. They would visit our clients at home, take precise measurements, help choose the right style, the lace trim from catalogue. Then, within two weeks the client would get a custom size bra. It would be fully made to order. This type of sale we are now trying to develop.

At the same time doing marketing research we noticed there were many start-ups functioning this way, interestingly, mostly targeting men. The clients of these start-ups are men buying sophisticated clothes.

Direct Sale

The growth in direct sales in the United States, is over 8 percent a year. It is a very interesting phenomenon, considering that for many people direct sale seems an outdated, bygone trend. Yet today's direct sale works differently than even a few years ago.

Nowadays women look for more flexible types of employment and making income. In the United States there is no guaranteed maternal leave that's why flexible forms of employment are so important. In our talks with Y Combinator we suggested that we not only wanted to offer bras but also a new quality of work for women.

Working in direct sales can turn out to be a very attractive solution for many women—mothers of young children, for students. At the same time a consultant selling specialized lingerie must be someone very professional, sensitive, and delicate. This work is very interesting, as it requires a personal connection with a client and advising her on many details. We are convinced that we will be able to realize our vision both in sales and in promoting our message of women's power.

We want to come back to Y Combinator and prove that we have succeeded.

***

The Interview Took Place on November 17, 2015 in San Francisco

CHAPTER 4

Contact IQ

API Address to the Brain of Every Employee

Kate Scisel comes from Kraków. She founded her first technology company at 22. Later she cooperated with a number of IT firms. One of her clients was the Californian start-up WhatsApp. She admits she was not able to understand at the time how such a small company could grow so much in such a short time.

In 2012, she decided to build her own start-up outside Poland. She moved to Berlin, London, and finally to Silicon Valley: "Silicon Valley did not seem like a logical choice for me but I still decided to move here and begin one of the most demanding stages of my life." At present Kate is developing her own start-up, Contact IQ. She told me about the complicated process of founding a start-up. She also addressed the issue of female founders in Silicon Valley.

Silicon Valley is a mix of dreamers who believe in the future. Many of them live in the future and are out of touch with the real world. Had they not been a bit "crazy" they would not have been able to overcome life's hurdles.

When I worked in Europe I read articles about the situation of women in Silicon Valley and I was somewhat surprised. I had the impression that they were either too sensitive or else they were blowing things out of proportion. But, unfortunately, my assumptions were wrong.

—Kate Scisel

I met with Kate in San Francisco at the Founders Den. This is short, pre-cise description of this place:

Founders Den is what could be termed a "startup heaven." But one problem: you gotta get invited to rent a desk here, so start networking!

Robert Scoble
blogger
Rackspace

The Kraków Start-up Ecosystem

We Did Not Know What a Start-up Was

I went to high school in Poland and Germany. When I returned to Kraków by chance I got a job at a technology company from New York. I helped in practically everything. Then my employer recommended me to a New York programmer with whom I started to collaborate. With this experience behind me in 2007, I established my first company managing server administration. It was a Polish-American firm. I was 21 and was still studying. From my university classes I went straight to the firm. It was a crazy time.

Most of our clients were in New York, and in Poland we hired special-ists to do the work. We administered the servers of some of the largest TV networks in the world.

At the time Amazon Web Services entered the market. We offered something similar, but our product was not fully scalable; it was, rather, an outsourcing service.

From the Polish perspective no one even dreamed of building global start-ups. Ten years ago we didn't even know what a start-up was!

Studies

I studied at Jagiellonian University. My studies were completely unre-lated to technology so I wanted to switch my major. My business partner, who also did not study software engineering, convinced me not to do it. He argued that in technology you have to be always up-to-date and at college they will teach me things that are already obsolete. I listened to his advice. Strangely enough all our best specialists studied philosophy, logic, or history. But they were passionate about programming and taught themselves to code.

New Challenges

Soon I was approached by a British company, Erlang Solutions (which employed some of the creators of the Erlang programming language). They asked me to set up and organize their Polish branch. I accepted their offer because I needed another challenge. For many months I traveled between Kraków and London. In addition to our office in Kraków we also had branches in Sweden and the UK.

Most of our contracts were covered by nondisclosure agreements, which was how it was done in Europe at the time. We were making innovative products but no one was supposed to know about it. There were no TechCrunch articles about us, no publicity.

The Time of Change

In those years no Polish university offered courses in Erlang. So our programmers started to teach that language to their professors at the AGH University of Science and Technology and in a few years Erlang was introduced to the university curriculum. The fact that programmers were teaching their professors felt impressive and indicative of the changing times. We started working with universities from all over Poland.

Erlang Programming Language

Erlang, which itself originated as a start-up, is currently being used by both small start-ups and large international corporations. Some of the major users are Ericsson, Facebook, WhatsApp, T-Mobile, and Goldman Sachs.

Meeting and cooperating with people who had invented a programming language used worldwide became a turning point in my career.

WhatsApp

My activity in those days you can describe as helping scalable start-ups. One of our clients was a budding start-up from Mountain View called

WhatsApp. When we started working with them they employed only four or five people.

We all know the story of WhatsApp. In 2014, it was sold to Facebook for 19 billion dollars! An almost unimaginable amount. In the tech industry in a very short time you can build up your company's value immensely. At present WhatsApp has about 800 million active users. And WhatsApp was not the only one of our clients that developed so fast!

What Is the Secret?

I watched our clients grow but I did not understand their secret. I saw business models where it didn't matter if the product had a few users or a few million users. I was full of admiration for our clients. As a witness to the process of product development, I knew how much stress it involved.

Today, as I look back on my fascination with the technology market, I can see how naïve I was. I could see how much could be gained. But I did not know the inside stories of how those companies who did not make it.

TEDxKraków

I remember how the Kraków start-up community was just emerging. In 2009, there was the first TEDxKraków meeting, which galvanized the Cracovian start-up ecosystem.

With just a few people, we organized TEDxKraków conference at practically zero cost. We got support from many people, we managed to find sponsors; we invited world-famous speakers. Jagiellonian University gave us use of a 500-seat room. That TEDx conference really energized Kraków.

The start-up ecosystem is so interconnected. Łukasz Kostka, who was then my roommate, met Jakub Krzych during the TEDx conference. Jakub's collaborator was at that time also Julia Krysztofiak. TEDx integrated the Kraków start-up community. Before people were creating interesting things but more privately, at home, individually. After that conference they began to network. The first *Hive53* community was created. And later the first Kraków Startup Weekend took place.

Risky Decision

In 2011, Erlang Solutions sold its shares. I think if our company had operated in Silicon Valley it would have enjoyed a much wider, global success. Exit in Europe was also a success, but not on the Valley scale.

I began to consider the next step in my life. I wanted to create something of my own. After having worked for a few years in tech, with world-class programmers, I could not imagine working in any other field. I got a few offers, but in the end I decided to leave Poland. I knew this was a risky decision. But I came to the conclusion that if I wanted to create a global company, I should do it outside Poland—which at the time lacked a solid system of innovation support.

Berlin, London, San Francisco

Key Criteria

I conducted an analysis of places where I could start my own operation. I did not want to make emotional decisions. I put all the data into an Excel spreadsheet. I chose the key criteria: a well-developed technology industry, good developers, and an innovation-friendly environment. I also wanted to work in a country whose language I was fluent in.

After completing my analysis I singled out three cities: Berlin, London, and San Francisco. I decided to travel to those three cities to find out how they functioned. At the time I thought this was a sensible plan. Today I think it was crazy.

Berlin

I moved for a month to Berlin. I got to know its start-up environment. I liked it there a lot. Still, I got the impression that it was a ground zero zone for *hype*. There was a lot of media noise around start-ups. This is exciting and attracts a lot of interesting, creative people. The best programmers are brought in from Poland.

And although Berlin is a fantastic place I decided not to do my start-up there.

London

My next destination was London. I also stayed there for a month. I worked at the London Google Campus. Just as with Berlin, London is a fantastic city, with great atmosphere but with the same problems as Berlin. First of all, they lacked programmers and just as in Germany, the few they had had been imported from Poland or other Eastern European countries. And of those, the best programmers were often lured into the London financial firms. London wasn't right either.

Mountain View

I described my journey on Facebook. My old Silicon Valley advisor got in touch and, expressing surprise, asked me what I was doing. When I told him about my plan he suggested that I come to San Francisco. I answered that I was going to Mountain View.

The Weather and the People Did it...

I came to Mountain View full of optimism. It was at the end of November, beginning of December. At this time of year, the weather is summer-like. I decided that, since San Francisco was so wonderful—climate-wise and people-wise—I was not leaving. My sister wrote to me that I could not stay in Silicon Valley just for the weather and the social life. I replied, "Just watch me!" And I stayed...

Moving into Silicon Valley was, in a way, contradicting my "European logic" since I was planning to employ programmers from Poland. The time difference between Poland and California is deadly for your sleep cycle. And, oddly enough, moving to Silicon Valley had never been my dream.

The Idea

The Search

In Silicon Valley I began collaborating with my former mentor. He told me that he would help because he had been helped by others in the past. For me it was an important gesture. I also contacted my old clients from Kraków. Every day I met new, great people. I started having new ideas and when I put them down on a piece of paper I realized the list was artificial. None of those projects was really my thing.

The Problem Found Me

Meeting so many people I was unable to keep track of so many names, business cards, and contacts. My network looked like a *disorganizational* mess. I knew a lot of people but I did not have access to them because their data were scattered, chaotic.

When I came to the Valley I had about three hundred Facebook friends. I don't know if it speaks to how many people we actually know. After moving to the Valley the number of my friends fast grew to 1,300. It was hard to analyze whom I had met, with whom I should meet again. I had contacts on Facebook, LinkedIn, in my e-mails. For the first time I encountered a problem which affected me personally; in fact, the problem found me, instead of the other way around.

Spreadsheet

I asked my future business partner, Peter, about how he organized all his contacts, business cards, telephone numbers. I knew he had a well-developed network. He told me he used Excel…

I peppered him with questions. What if someone changes their job and moves from one company to another? What about the people that you contacted via e-mail? There were no good answers. If someone doesn't update their Facebook or LinkedIn profile or doesn't have one, then the contact with that person is lost.

We agreed it was a problem looking for a solution.

Prototype

I came up with the idea of a mobile app that would organize all contacts. The principle was simple: after entering a name and surname we should get all the professional information about that person. I started preparing the application prototype. For the first several weeks I worked alone and in six months the prototype was ready. Then Peter decided it was time to develop the product. He quit a well-paying job and took a risk of coming in with me.

The First Product

We decided to pull together all our contacts—from the Facebook and LinkedIn accounts, from e-mails, all applications that we used. In this way we created a spreadsheet containing information on all people from our accounts. We started adding functions and macros, fine-tuning the data. Finally, from that chaotic list we made a product.

The Team

We were a two-person team. We needed a really talented technical leader—an engineer that would be our CTO. We did not want to recruit, but rather just to meet the right person. We looked through all our contacts. It was the first test of our product.

Local start-ups in the early stage do not advertise their hiring. No one organizes interviews. Start-ups just don't do it this way.

Google was established by two friends who knew and liked each other and worked well together—Sergey and Larry. They build the prototype of their product together. They consulted with their Stanford professor and employed a bunch of their friends. This way, they kept extending their network. For the first years that's how Google functioned. People recommended one another, creating a base built on trust. The base of Contact IQ is the same.

From the European point of view someone would say that looking for employees among your friends is nepotism. But from the point of view in Silicon Valley such a strategy is seen as enterprising and efficient. This is how we found Daniel Mendalka who came to San Francisco for Google I/O conference. Today Daniel is one of the founders of our start-up.

Cease and Desist

Court Summons

In 2013, we were sued by AOL for using data available on Creative Commons. We received a Cease and Desist letter. On Thursday we put our application in the App Store and on following Monday we were summoned to court. I could not believe it!

I was sure that we had not broken any law and I ignored the summons. Soon we received another letter, written in aggressive, lawyerly jargon. We could see this was no joke.

AOL is a gigantic corporation, and owner of TechCrunch which in turn owns CrunchBase. Both companies form a database that had the Creative Commons license with the so-called BY condition. This meant that as long as the source was quoted, everyone could use their content for free.

Wired Magazine

We were contacted by David Kravets, a well-known journalist of the prestigious magazine *Wired*. He said he knew about our case and was writing a story about it. We were very surprised. The question was simple—why would a huge corporation, using half-truths, try to destroy a start-up? It is to prevent situations like that that the Creative Commons organization was established in the first place.

When *Wired* magazine published the article telling our story, other media also reported it. We found out that media narratives cannot be controlled.

Let's Fight!

We could have given up and closed our company or we could fight. We decided to fight!

Conflict of Interest

We contacted our lawyer, one of the best in Silicon Valley. He had represented Zappos during its sale to Amazon.

The lawyer said he would have helped us but he couldn't. Since AOL is the client of the majority of law firms in Silicon Valley, the conflict of interest made him and other lawyers refuse us their services.

Electronic Frontier Foundation (EFF)

So we turned to Electronic Frontier Foundation (EFF). This organization, if it takes on a case, does so pro bono. The Foundation representatives decided our case was vital not just for our company but also for the cause of Internet freedom.

Thanks to Electronic Frontier we won. The trial lasted a few months and cost our firm a lot of irrevocably lost time. But in the end we received a free license for the use of the database. The conflict around our company taught us a great lesson. We understood, among other things, why people pay so much for database access.

Development

Contact IQ

From a consumer application we started to turn into a B2B product. We named it Contact IQ.

Corporate Rolodex

One of the greatest challenges that faces the founder is to develop a good sales pitch. Initially we described Contact IQ as a *graph search* for business but none of our nontechnical friends understood what that was. One of our users defined our product as a *corporate rolodex*. The phrase turned out to be catchy and accurate. That's why we decided to borrow this name. The shortest description of Contact IQ is: *Private secure corporate rolodex for your company.*

API Address for the Company's Brain

If you asked me who I know at Google I could name maybe five people. If I added additional data—someone I know who also worked for Twitter and lived in San Francisco—I could not answer that question because it contains too many criteria.

Our brain automatically searches information about the people who are close to us or whom we met recently. This is how our mind works. Human brains cannot actively search information containing more than about 250 contacts. Working on our product, we wanted to create something that was analogous to an API[1] address to the company's "brain." Such a product had not been created before.

We Do Not Yet Have Access to Such Intelligence

In Contact IQ, we created a system that collects these data and can analyze it in real time. Companies use our system when they want to, for example, find an ideal client. The system can also be useful when you search for CEOs of an industry living in San Francisco or try to contact representatives of particular companies, for example, in New York. It also facilitates whom we know as an organization and how we are connected to them.

The First Client

In the initial stages of our start-up my partner and I were able to finance it ourselves because we had previously sold our own companies. First we wanted to determine if our product made sense and only then start to think about financing.

Our first client bought five licenses of our product for 500 dollars. The sale came to me on its own! I was having coffee with my laptop open and working when someone asked me what I was doing. I told him and when he asked me the price, I did not know what to answer—I did not want to spoil my first sale!

We got more and more paying clients. Then I realized that since users were prepared to pay for an unfinished product it meant we were on to something. Every founder is afraid of charging first clients and I was, in a sense, still ashamed of the product—it still lacked an intuitive interface and a good website. But the clients saw value in it even at that early stage—which was encouraging.

And I had not yet chosen the color palette...

---

[1] API: In computer programming, an Application Programming Interface (API) is a set of subroutine definitions, protocols, and tools for building application software. In general terms, it is a set of clearly defined methods of communication between various software components. (Source: Wikipedia).

It Was a Bit Daunting

Our first client invited his friends to Contact IQ. In this way many influential Silicon Valley people added their contacts to our system. At first I was a little daunted. I was worried the system would crash. I was leery of negative opinions. But clients just kept using the product while we worked on it. The Contact IQ network kept growing fast.

Investors

We learned a lot from our first client. One of our first investments we got from him. It wasn't the largest check of those we had received, but it meant a lot to us.

We also raised a small seed round. Our investors were private individuals, people connected to Google or PayPal. They were from an external network. A few investors found us on their own and offered financing—these are always very important moments to us.

Founding Team

The initial period of establishing a start-up is so intense that the people involved in product development must share mutual understanding and honesty. There is too much going on each day. If we were choosing people just for their competence the start-up would fall apart immediately. I was extremely lucky with my partners. Both Daniel and Peter are guys with whom I can talk about anything; we use constructive criticism. What's most important for a budding start-up are well functioning basic human relations such as trust and respect. If people working in a team don't like spending time together their start-up has a slim chance of survival. Initially the founders should spend time in one physical space. In our case we also lived in the same apartment.

I would like our first 20 employees to also feel that they are a part of the founding team. We try for every worker to have a real impact on Contact IQ. We want our staff to feel comfortable about voicing their opinions. In the United States, workers often own shares of the companies for which they work. What's good for the firm is good for them. In Contact IQ, we also give shares to our team members.

At present we are opening a branch in Poland. And although there are not too many female programmers on the market, in Contact IQ we want to meet them. Employing a woman would bring balance to our team.

Female Founders

Women in Tech Sector

We are opening Pandora's box… Women in tech is a very sensitive subject. When I worked in Europe I read articles on the situation of women in Silicon Valley and was somewhat surprised. I had the impression that the women in Silicon Valley must be either delicate flowers or that they exaggerate the problems. Working in Poland and in London I never encountered such degree of gender discrimination.

They Exaggerate?

After living in Silicon Valley for the first few months, I was dazzled by it. I had heard of how female founders were treated but I did not quite believe those stories. I thought girls should spend more time developing the product and then they would not have trouble raising a financial round or finding mentors. Only after a few months of work did I start to witness many awkward situations.

The First Disappointment

I was incorrect in thinking that women in Silicon Valley were treated on a par with men. Starting with mentoring, women do not have equal opportunity because the passage of knowledge across gender lines is harder. Often it gives rise to insinuations and ambiguous situations. My first disillusionment came when my good friend, a CEO of a large company, refused to mentor our start-up. I was not just surprised but disappointed. I did not understand his decision. I received an official e-mail in which he wrote that for reasons of his involvement in many boards of directors and lack of time he could not work with me. In spite of the e-mail his attitude toward me did not change his—he called me regularly on the phone and unofficially advised me with my start-up. But only unofficially.

Recently he apologized. He said he could not be my mentor because I was an attractive young woman and he did not want to give rise to unnecessary gossip. Besides he also promised his wife that he would not mentor women after work hours.

That was the most painful compliment I ever got.

That situation made me wonder about the status of women in the male-dominated world of technology.

Mentors are concerned about how their social environment will react. Will the wife agree that the husband meets up with "some blonde" after hours? And without mentors there is no support. Who, if not a mentor, will recommend us to investors at the early stage of our business? This creates a vicious circle that we need to break.

A Complex Problem

Many men mean well, they just don't know many women who run start-ups. Some of them use their position to get to know a woman better and since sometimes they don't know how to invite a girl out to dinner they write an e-mail: "Hey, let's talk about your start-up." Female founders often think that someone "important" is interested in their work while in fact they are interested in them personally. Such situations cause many misunderstandings. I don't know how to solve this problem.

Industry Meetings

Many times I was asked with whom I came to a meeting—assuming I was accompanying a man—while I came to an industry meeting because of my work and I am a founder of a tech start-up. Many times I was asked to serve a drink, assuming I was a hostess.

Initially I didn't think much about these little misunderstandings. I gave up wearing black to such conferences because most hostesses wear black.

One time my friend and I were invited to a group photo. She is a senior executive in one of the biggest Silicon Valley companies. It turned out they thought we were hostesses hired for photo ops. I just laughed but my friend was very offended.

Tolerance?

Theoretically Silicon Valley has a great culture of tolerance and mutual respect. In practice it is not always the case. If a woman does not want to be misunderstood she should refrain from doing many seemingly innocuous things. After arriving from Europe for the first months I wore dresses. Until the moment when I was told that I could not come to meetings in a dress, as it constituted "sending a signal." From then on I stopped wearing dresses. Now I only wear jeans and T-shirts.

Recently I read an article whose author—a female programmer—noticed that when she went to a conference in a dress people took her for a hostess. When the next day she went to the same conference wearing pants and a T-shirt people would talk business with her. This is not caused by bad intentions. It is just stereotypical thinking.

Pay it Forward in Silicon Valley

Getting financing is hard on everyone but if a founder is a woman things can be double hard. The market keeps getting information about new start-ups closing financial rounds. Such start-ups are often established by people with previous successes. They have an established network, they have worked with influential persons. Looking for financing, they turn to people with whom they have already cooperated and now they are harvesting their share of Silicon Valley's "pay it forward." The investors can see clearly in whom and in what they are investing. In Silicon Valley there are many situations that are completely illogical from the European perspective.

Questions

During meetings with investors a male founder will be asked about technical details while a woman gets questions connected to marketing. It is an artificial approach, but unfortunately very common.

Women get asked: *What do you think about it from a female perspective?* —although my product is not targeted just at women.

Events for Women

I usually am against extremes and organizing women-only events are in my view an extreme measure. On the other hand you have to start somewhere. Women's organizations do so much good that one should not criticize their work. If thanks to such support groups it will be easier for women to find mentors this is the first step in the right direction. Women can recommend each other to others, not just women. It is important for women to speak up. I think that women often are scared to address certain matters in the presence of men. I took part in several conferences organized for female founders and indeed the conversations in those meetings were different.

A Place of Talent Honing

Dreamers Believing in the Future

Silicon Valley is a Mecca for dreamers where many different cultures coexist and cooperate. The Valley attracts positive thinkers. People hearing even the craziest idea will imagine how to make it happen. Silicon Valley is a hub for dreamers who believe in the future. Many of them live in the future and are out of touch with the real world. Had they not been a bit crazy they would not have been able to overcome hurdles. People here are optimistic although everyday work here is hard and the real estate market is among the most expensive in the world.

To Get Started Here…

Start-ups operating in Poland should start looking for American clients on the Internet. They should have a Minimum Viable Product (MVP) and have income before coming to the Valley for the living expenses. Do not start with looking for an investor in the Valley. To become a part of the local environment you should build your network. If you talk with someone who doesn't know you the conversation will be very diplomatic and you will not receive any valuable, unfiltered information from them.

Working for a Large Company

It is worth considering coming to Silicon Valley for several months to work for a large company, get to know the local ecosystem, and help out other start-ups. Then, launching your own start-up you are already a part of the local community. Also, getting a visa is easier and less costly when a company like Facebook or Google takes care of it. Maybe my advice is not for everyone. Still, I think that young Polish people are so well organized that if they want to come here they can do it.

Feedback

Every moment is a good to start a conquest of the world. You should just remember that a Warsaw client is different from an American client. What matters for the Europeans can be irrelevant to the Americans.

In Contact IQ we work with a very sensitive product. Companies hand us their data and this is our added value. We have a client in London and the feedback we get from him is very different from the one we get from our clients in the United States.

You Must Unlearn What You Have Learned

Coming from Poland to Silicon Valley it would be good to forget all you learned working with the European market. This is hard. Here in the Valley, it is important to be open to new information. And instead of starting with complaints it is best to try and understand the local community and its rules. Before coming to the Valley I lived in many countries—Germany, England, Australia—but figuring out the specifics of Silicon Valley took me six months. This place escapes logical analysis. And founders tend to logically analyze a situation. Investors often don't invest logically, they use various criteria for their choices. Silicon Valley has a gigantic accumulation of capital. It is inhabited by successful people who want to invest their own money. And understanding the motives behind an investor's decision can be very hard.

The Client Is Crucial

When a start-up gets its first clients some problems are likely to be solved. Twitter survived in spite of many obstacles. Same with Uber[2]—it fought many battles and had the product not enjoyed clients' support it would have disappeared long ago. That's why the clients are crucial. Start-ups offering consumer products have a harder time making income. This kind of operation needs a different plan as there is no simple way to predict company growth.

Founders Den

In Contact IQ we never went through an accelerator. As a start-up we are members of Founders Den—"an association for experienced entrepreneurs." Founders Den was established by Jonathan Abrams, the founder of Friendster.

Every six months Founders Den accepts a few new start-ups—they can work there, and have access to such mentors as Keith Rabois or Dennis Crowley. The list of mentors is impressive. To get into Founders Den you have to be recommended by an existing member or a mentor. I was recommended by the founder of AngelList. I was lucky to have met many outstanding people in the course of my work; people who created global products on world scale. Every one of them is an inspiration for me.

On Success

Global Product

Success in Silicon Valley means creating a product which will change the world and make life better. Will it be a product that will give people more time, income, information? People here believe that they can curve the space-time continuum and change the world. For me success means making a global product that is scalable.

---

[2] The interview was conducted in July 2015, meantime Uber underwent some internal changes.

Visa 01

I am not just a woman-founder. I am also a foreigner, an immigrant. Luckily there are many immigrants in Silicon Valley. Last year I was granted working visa O1.[3] This is my personal success, as well as the success of our company. The investors started treating us more seriously. Now we don't have to worry about bureaucratic matters unconnected to our work.

A Milestone

Coming to Silicon Valley and competing with other local companies.

Feedingforward.com

I am often a judge at hackathons. During an event last year the judges were very critical of an idea presented by a young woman who did not have a finished product, just a vision. I could see that she took that criticism very personally. And hackathons are supposed to be creative, joyful events and not merciless criticism.

After the presentation I came up to her and told her that the judges did not understand her and had given her unfair feedback. I told her to keep developing her project. The girl had found the problem she wanted to tackle. Every day in the United States, tons of food gets thrown out while 49 million Americans go hungry. Why does the country that wastes so much food have so many hungry people? The girl decided to solve the problem and connect the two worlds. She decided to take food from those who discard it and give it to those in need.

Today feedingforward.com[4] feeds almost a million people.

To me this is a true success story. And to think that thoughtless criticism almost killed that project before it even got born. You have to

---

[3] *The O-1 nonimmigrant visa is for the individual who possesses extraordinary ability in the sciences, arts, education, business, or athletics, or who has a demonstrated record of extraordinary achievement in the motion picture or television industry and has been recognized nationally or internationally for those achievements. (Source: www.uscis.gov).*

[4] Now: Copia.

remember that the person who presents a new idea sees it and imagines it differently. And the listeners have to hear it with the ears of a storyteller's audience.

Failures

Admitting defeat is painful. Creating a start-up involves many people—founders, investors, employees, partners. In the Valley we witness many successes so admitting a failure is especially hard. The slogan *It's OK to fail* is misunderstood. Under no circumstance is it "OK" to fail, as failing involves disappointing many people who count on us: co-founders, investors, clients, workers, and so on.

It's OK to fail means that failures happen and you have to minimize their consequences. If you can save something for the investors you have to give it back to them. If you can pass your clients to another firm you should make this transfer ASAP. That's why it seems critical that if the company is going to fail you should speed up this process. However, failures often are precursors to success. Silicon Valley certainly does not encourage failure. But Silicon Valley promotes risk. And when risk is combined with innovation failures are inevitable. If founders and investors did not risk the business would become very predictable and there would be no Google, Uber, or Facebook.

I know it Has to Work

We can never be sure that what we do will not turn into failure. That's why I treat every activity as a challenge. At Contact IQ we put all our eggs in one basket. My work visa is connected to the company. If the company is not successful I will go back to Europe. That's why I am even more aware that *it's NOT OK to fail.* I know it has to work.

***

The interview took place on July 2, 2015 in San Francisco.

CHAPTER 5

Moiseum, DailyArt

For the Love of Art

Zuzanna Stańska, museum lover.

She goes against the grain and challenges the status quo.

For start-ups she gave up her steady job. She became a professional champion of art.

She introduces innovation to museum galleries. She is the author of many novel initiatives. She organizes meetings for museum community and for art lovers.

She studied art history and international relations at Warsaw University and received an Erasmus scholarship. She featured in a BBC 30 Under 30 story showing 30 women who were successful in running a global business.

She is based in Warsaw. She travels to Silicon Valley on vacations and to learn. In August 2015, she revisited Silicon Valley and also went to Burning Man festival. With youthful enthusiasm she tells stories about important matters—running a company, responsibility and the meaning of art in our everyday life.

It seems to me that the Europeans have a kind of inferiority complex in relation to art. While talking about art people stress their education, worldliness.

In the United States people come to a museum to listen to lectures during which they ask questions, get answers, participate in discussions. They create a community. For the Americans art does not mean haughty discussion. Art is something worth knowing about, worth learning new things about, as art is an integral part of our civilization, part of our everyday life.

—**Zuzanna Stańska**

First Startup Weekend

Musei Capitolini

In 2010, as part of Erasmus program, I got placed at the Capitolini Museum in Rome. It has many "boring" antiquity artifacts. I was accepted as an intern to their IT section. My boss was an archeologist whose ambition was the introduction of new technologies in the museum.

For three months I copied data from PDF files to the database and that was my whole range of duties. Yet I was able to learn a lot about applications and technological solutions for smartphones. In those days smartphones, especially in Poland, were just beginning to gain popularity. I returned to Poland intrigued and curious about new technologies and innovative solutions for mobile devices.

What, I Cannot Manage?

I began to be interested in technological solutions for use in museums. At the same time I was also looking for a mission for myself and my life. I started a blog on technologies in museums and decided to write a BA thesis on history of art.

In Warsaw it was the time of a real start-up boom. Many of my friends got involved in those enterprises. There was a talk of a rush of investors into Warsaw. In March 2011, Warsaw held its first Polish Startup Weekend. One of the organizers, Kamila Sidor, was looking for someone to help operate the camera and suggested that I take up this "challenge." My friend presented the job as something needing a world-class cinematographer such as Janusz Kamiński… That's why I wondered if I could do it and if I could afford to take a break from my course work. It was the end of the semester and I was studying at two faculties. The same person told me I would not do well with start-ups since I did not know that community. Then I decided to go! Out of spirit of defiance: "What, I cannot manage?! Not good enough—who, me?"

Startup Weekend

I did a good job with the camera and, what's more important, I made new contacts. Startup Weekend was superbly organized and the whole event was broadcast online. It was the first meeting integrating the start-up industry in Poland. It was the first time that people who represented a similar way of thinking, worked with similar problems, had similar ideas, read TechCrunch but did not know one another previously and were able to connect.

A Milestone

Warsaw Startup Weekend turned my life around. The fact that I went there and got to know the community where I felt at home was critical for my future career. Had I not been told that I was not good enough for start-ups I would probably be somewhere else today, doing something else.

First Job

It was during Warsaw Startup Weekend that Kamila Sidor asked me to become Community Manager at a fund, which, like California's Y Combinator—created Poland's first accelerator for start-ups. In this way I started my training and soon I began working there full time. That was the only full-time job I've ever held. I worked for almost a year. I got to know the start-up community and understood what working there was all about and what these people were doing.

At the same time I started working with museums. I tried to interest them in mobile applications and using applications in museums. I don't know why I was so intrigued by mobile applications—maybe because I always have my phone with me. I never part with it.

Moiseum and Daily Art

First Client

When I got my first client I said goodbye to the Fund and started a company called Moiseum. It was in 2012. My first client was Museum of the History of Polish Jews. But I had no idea how to run a business! That's why for a long time nothing was going on in my company. It took nine months for Moiseum to start full operation and 12 months for the market to be ready for the projects I developed.

I Was Not an Expert on Mobile Apps

After several months of stagnation I used the rest of the money to create the DailyArt app, which, to my great surprise, did very well on the market. I was very lucky. When I started designing DailyArt I was not an expert on mobile applications. I knew neither how to make them nor how to promote them. I did not know how to sell them, how to talk to people, how to find clients. I did not know how to create a product that will be both catchy and well received by the users and market. I had no idea how to go about creating a start-up. In one word, I knew nothing! Still, I was successful and I find it completely unbelievable. Moiseum has clients, DailyArt works. Everything happened by complete accident.

Moiseum

Starting up with Moiseum I assumed I would be making ready-made applications for museums. You can do this in many ways—I decided on a consulting version, although financing mobile apps is for many museums a serious financial burden.

How Moiseum Works

I prepare individual products for museums, meet with museum workers, and spend long hours talking with them. I find out whom they want to reach, what they expect from me and what their budget is. I gather all the information and prepare a proposal which is unique and answers the particular needs of a given team and is aimed at a particular museum visitor. I suggest unique solutions. If a museum wants to introduce an audio tour I can prepare an app facilitating the walk through the building. We created such a project for The Museum of King John III's Palace at Wilanów, in Warsaw.

I can also prepare a mobile version of the product which accompanies the traditional paper version—this is what we did for The Warsaw Uprising Museum. In this case the museum was using only printed maps, which was not efficient. My team prepared mobile maps, which visitors could easily install on their phones.

I Learn All the Time

Only now, after more than two years from the launch of the first version of DailyArt am I beginning to understand how the whole mechanism worked. I read a lot and talk to people and on this basis I try to reverse engineer what happened. Especially since I am planning to build the next, more advanced version of DailyArt.

Of course it took more than a couple of months to create a successful mobile application. My learning took a long time, in stages, while doing a range of projects.

One Story a Day...

A successful product is a combination of the idea, its execution, and teamwork. In the case of a mobile application what is crucial is the content delivered to the user. The rest is just "bells and whistles." My application delivers one work of art a day, which for the users is the source of inspiration. It also teaches kids to interact with art. It is an escape from mundane matters. My recipient can pride himself on his knowledge of art, can use it as a conversation starter. He can boost his popularity a bit. It all starts with one story a day. DailyArt provides the story. Only one story... or maybe as much as one story...

Dailyart Is My Shield

The DailyArt app was a success. I don't need to be modest. I am getting excellent feedback from thousands of users. The awareness that DailyArt enhances the lives of thousands of people all around the globe is amazing and empowers me to keep going.

DailyArt PRO

The paid version of DailyArt—DailyArt PRO—makes money. Initially I thought no one would ever buy it! Such thinking is my Polish sin... I thought the application needed to be free because art itself should be free.

Today there are two version available—free DailyArt and paid DailyArt PRO.

I decided to start the paid version to collect money via crowdfunding. I needed money for my living expenses. People pitched in and I could focus on work. And the cost of making a spin-off was minimal. In the beginning the paid version cost one dollar. I soon realized that even the most banal applications related to art are usually more expensive. And DailyArt PRO is an educational app, a valuable one, carrying a message and developing. That's why I raised the price to five dollars.

I was dumb not to have capitalized on this app as much as I could have. Now we are developing a new version of DailyArt, which will be better in the look and functionality, as well as bringing in more income. I learned from my mistakes.

More on Crowdfunding

I turned to crowdfunding as it was the fastest way to raise extra money. My application had already over 20,000 users. And that was just the beginning. I wanted to raise a small amount, just a few thousand dollars. I assumed that it would not be hard. That was all that mattered. I might use crowdfunding in the future again, as I have a strong user base—over 200 thousand active users, including some "psychofans." I think at this stage the fundraising campaign is relatively easy. More important, I don't have to worry about finding investors.

Innovative Initiatives and Meetings

Slow Art Day

Slow Art Day was my first individual project. I first read about the international version of Slow Art Day on Twitter, just before my first Warsaw Startup Weekend. I also decided to create a similar event in Poland. It worked out very well and became an annual gig that's gaining in popularity.

In America on Slow Art Day you visit a museum at a certain hour, viewing five pieces of art of your choice and then discussing them.

But I think in Poland such a model would not catch on because people are generally afraid of museums and ashamed of their own ignorance. They are afraid of being ridiculed and looking silly. So as a result they would not be able to focus for even 30 seconds on a painting and they would be wondering if they had chosen the right one. That's why I decided to choose those five pieces myself. The animators initiate discussions around those specific pieces. This creates a sure sequence that the participants can follow. So the walkthrough becomes more user-friendly, not so intimidating and alien. And meanwhile the animator tells a story of a particular painting, warming up the atmosphere. This is something half-way between a standard museum visit and the original version of the Slow Art Day.

We Are Museums

This year, unfortunately, I did not have time to co-organize the *We are museums* conference. For me it started in 2012, with meeting a young French woman who promotes museums. I do the same through my application; and she makes movies, writes blogs and other social events. We both believe that museums should be people-friendly. I decided to help her. We cooperated at a campaign *We are museums* in Lithuania and a year later in Poland.

I Can Only Help

I have such a spirit of contradiction that I always go against the grain although making a revolution is never my goal. I just keep thinking and conclude that certain things need to change. I push for changes. If five years ago someone else had invented or organized Moiseum I would have joined the project and would have wanted to work on it.

This is what happened with the *We are museums* campaign. It was neither my idea nor my initiative but I could lend a hand so I did. My actions will not change the world; I can only help. *We are museums* is a worthwhile project so I decided to get involved.

Metamuzeum

During the *We are museums* campaign, as it was, the Polish museum community had no space where people could meet, gossip, and share ideas in an informal, easy atmosphere. There were only scientific conferences during which there were no socializing opportunities such as a before or an after party. I came to the conclusion that the lack of a developed network was hurting this community. Museum workers do not cultivate friendships and, changing posts, lose contact. But they could learn so much from one another! This is what sparked the idea of Metamuzeum. It was supposed to integrate the community. By creating Metamuzeum I wanted those who were active, or wanted to be active, those who were looking for work or would like to get to know the community but had no place to go—to meet in one venue and talk over a beer.

A Breath of Fresh Air

I started organizing gatherings integrating the community and offered workshops and eventully initiated meetups for museum workers.

I am also working on social media events aiming at promoting museums or creating new channels of communication with actual or potential visitors.

These are small things but in the museum environment they are like a breath of fresh air.

The Team

I Always Did Things Myself

I keep learning not to do everything myself. Our team works remotely. We communicate via Facebook and Slack, sometimes via e-mail. Thanks to my trainee I have learned to delegate tasks. For the first few years I couldn't afford an employee. I always did things myself. Now I don't have a big team. I cooperate with three mobile developers, one graphic designer, a WordPress expert and I employ Justyna, my assistant. These are the people I can always turn to and I know I can rely on their work. The number of people involved in a project depends on the job. I can delegate only "soft" tasks that I do every day. The rest of company activities require special skills. The graphic designer does his part, the programmers their part.

How to Start

In the beginning you need a good team. I've had enormous luck with people. I've been working with the same team for over two years. I know they will not cheat me. They will give good advice. We are very honest with one another.

One also needs a well-prepared MVP (minimum viable product). We need to know if our idea will fly or not. I feel I won a lottery ticket because I have natural PR skills. I could write e-mails that made it to the press—the media picked up my ideas. I got some publicity. These are two fundamental things.

You also need a good product. DailyArt application became popular when it had the ugliest imaginable graphics. The first version of the application was atrocious; it crashed and did not really work. In spite of those serious imperfections the market picked up the idea, the app became popular and got many users. That's why the idea is so important—what matters most is what the app does and what are its uses, not the looks. My application looked terrible…

Shares or Salary?

Many start-up founders believe that initially you have to give your employees company shares. This is supposed to encourage the team to work on the new idea. In my opinion this doesn't work. None of my employees has shares in Moiseum. I am a sole proprietor; it's not a company.

The first two people with whom I worked were my friends. I knew them socially. When I was creating my team I already had clients and I could pay my guys for their work. In addition, working for Moiseum is inspiring. It does not consist of churning out another standard application but it contributes to the arts, culture, education. Our work is very creative and brings great satisfaction.

I Just Appreciate Them

I never omit or diminish the contributions that my collaborators brought to the project. I always mention all persons involved by name and I officially thank them, which, interestingly, is not a standard approach and does not always happen. In every application developed by our team we always list everybody and include the links to their LinkedIn or Facebook profiles. I just appreciate people with whom I work. All my later collaborators were recommended by my two first coworkers. They had worked together on other projects and together moved to the next ones. I am friends with all people with whom I work. It would be impossible for me not to like people with whom I collaborate and not to be their friend.

Experiences in Running Start-ups

Financing?

Unfortunately, my experiences with investors have been bad. When I was starting up with Moiseum and DailyArt I thought I needed an investor. I even went into talks with one of them but, luckily, I did not work with him. It turned out my would be investor had no funds. He took me on a wild goose chase for four months and at the same time he used my app DailyArt to promote his own program. That specific "investor" managed to harm many other young start-ups.

That's why I am afraid of investors. I worked for one of them and I got to know the Polish realities. I know the investor market in Poland. I also am clear that I would not like to participate in the investor market in the United States. I prefer to work my own way, with my own money and not burden others with my bad decisions.

In any case, at present Moiseum functions well enough not to need any external financing.

There Is Much More To Do...

Theoretically I could cooperate with any museum in the world. But for every market you need a network of people and contacts. If you offer a product that requires consulting, you have to form relationships and be very professional. This is how it works all over the world.

It takes a lot of time to create business relations and construct a product. That's why conquering other markets or taking my product to international museums is not scalable for me at the moment, especially if entering those markets is to turn a profit. That's why I prefer to concentrate on developing DailyArt, which is an attractive global product. It helps me to work effectively in the Polish market. I can look after local museums. And there is a lot to do in Poland. It took me three years to get to know the environment, to meet the people, promote myself and my work. And this is just Poland with only a population of 38 million.

Competition?

My competitors are creative agencies, which sometimes try to break into the museum community. To be honest, these are usually quite harmful activities. There is no big company on the market that would be likely to specialize in museums because, frankly, working with museums is a pain. The circumstance where you have several employees on a payroll and enough clients to pay for it is almost impossible in Poland. All the agencies that planned to work just with museums had to eventually widen their offer, as they couldn't make a living from such a narrow specialty.

The Best Part of This Work

… is when I get another DailyArt review. Someone writes that every day he reads the picture description to his four-year old daughter and they dream of one day going to a museum and looking at that particular piece of art. It touches me deeply when I read such stories.

It is when I meet someone who says that he just downloaded the app on his phone or tablet and uses it every day. It's a wonderful feeling.

The Most Stressful and the Hardest Part

The money. In the beginning I sometimes had it, sometimes I didn't. I organized my work in such a way that I don't need to worry about paying my team. My team salaries have always been written into the projects. But supporting myself and my cat… paying the bills—that involved pressure. I had to learn to deal with the financial as well as the psychological burden. There were times when I did not have money and I knew there were no commissions on the horizon. Those were dreadful times.

I think about those founders who like to take ten million dollars in financing and then "burn" it—there are many such stories in Silicon Valley. I heard many of them when I took part in the Female Founders program at Blackbox. One of the participants confessed to crying at night because her start-up had just two million dollars left which was enough money for the next three months. She was paying herself a 3,000 dollar salary. Three thousand dollars in Silicon Valley? This is nothing. I cannot imagine the level of stress of that woman. It had to be absurd. Such model of operation makes no sense. You cannot do it on the long run.

What I Like Most About Start-ups...

...are the people. I wouldn't stay in the start-up community but I love the people. They are wonderful. They are open, they want to learn, they understand the world, they have their passions. I am 27 and I can see that my college friends stopped in their tracks, got stuck at a certain stage of their life. And I cannot find a common language with them anymore. That's why I go to conferences and get involved in the start-up life— because the people are so great.

The Culture of Defeat

The start-up community practices mutual support. Every start-upper knows that even if we don't succeed we have the culture of defeat to back us up. Setbacks are accepted by the community and sometimes they are even useful. You have to pick yourself up and keep going. You have to pat each other on the back and start another project. Start-up people learn from their mistakes and this is a valuable lesson. In other industries there is not so much mutual support and understanding for failures.

Sources of Knowledge

Knowledge is essential. You can get it in many ways, but certainly not through EU or government programs, rarely through incubators or accelerators. To be honest, except for Y Combinator and 500 Start-ups, accelerators don't make sense. You can find a lot on the Internet. I spend a few hours every day doing research online. There is a lot of content and a lot of wisdom. Of course, many people try to promote themselves online. But if someone starts to talk nonsense it quickly becomes apparent. You need to filter critically, but through independent reading you can learn a lot. All kinds of industry meetings are also very useful. One needs direct interactions with people. It can be a Startup Weekend or an *after party* at a conference or a themed meetup. These are all important sources of knowledge.

Simple Principle of Global Scope

You should think globally from day one. It doesn't make sense to act otherwise. If I first created DailyArt just in Polish I would have gotten nowhere and I would be stuck to this day. The rule of global scope from the start does not apply exclusive to art applications—it applies to many other services. The market in Poland is too small. There is no reason not to start globally. What does it mean—globally? Globally means in English. You should start with that from the very beginning. It is a very simple principle.

When a Start-up Ceases To Be a Start-up?

When it starts making money. Some serious money.

On Work–Life Balance

Work Is My Life

I cannot work nonstop, at some point my brain turns itself off. I must go out and talk with friends, go to the movies, read a book, watch a show. There are some days when I start working first thing in the morning and at 2 p.m. I need a *power nap*. After waking up I can keep clicking. I could not manage working 10+ hours a day. My body would rebel. I know there are programmers who can code nonstop for 18 hours. I can't do that. I will never be able to do that, so I stopped trying.

I don't fall into depression because I let myself rest—I need to take breaks as otherwise I would not be able to go on. But naturally, I think about work all the time. I surround myself with industry people; the work is always present. It's my life.

I Would Like…

…for all my projects to go exactly as I planned them. I would like to have the financial freedom to create new projects. And most of my projects are nonprofit. Apparently this is how it goes. I have never aspired to a marble palace and a Porsche… that does not mean that I would say no to a good car; but I am not going to martyr myself in the name of material wealth.

The Measure of Success or Luxury?

Currently I am involved in projects that I really care about. It all came together last year. First, I really wanted to work for The Warsaw Rising Museum. Second, I wanted to create an application for blind people. In future I would like to make an application for children and seniors. Those applications will be tailored to the particular needs of those two social groups.

These are my measures of success. I would like to work with competent institutions on interesting projects. But it is also a measure of luxury.

Biggest Success

Surviving the last three years! Now I have reached a turning point and I know nothing really bad can happen anymore. The worst already happened and passed. I survived the time of having no clients and no precise plan for the future. Moiseum has been up and running for over three years. I can manage, I have my little nest, I have clients, I know how to go forward. DailyArt has a great potential and I know how I want to develop it.

These are my biggest successes.

One of the Few Girls

I have never felt successful. I cannot even compare myself to many Polish founders who really made it big. I am still far behind many start-uppers who built impressive companies.

My Personal Failure

I did not finish my Master's thesis. Although now I don't need it for anything. My supervisor asked me to rewrite the finished text. But I gave up. I never submitted the paper. This is my failure.

Inspirations

I have no master. Still, I know some people who inspire and motivate me—both in life and professionally, and these two areas are parallel for me. I am motivated by close people who run their lives their own way—I draw on their everyday life successes. I think it is fantastic that someone has their own opinion and keeps realizing their own goals. These are the people that inspire me. Sometimes they make mistakes but the mistakes are also a source of inspiration.

Dad Gave Me Freedom

People would usually give me bad advice. Suggestions such as: study something sensible, otherwise you will not get a job at KPMG. When I started studying art history I was told I was mad since with such a degree I would live under a bridge!

Luckily, my close family, namely my father, never tried to give me directions. He was sure I could cope. He knew I would find the right way, my way. He did not give me verbal advice but I've always felt he was supporting me. I knew I could do what I wanted, how I wanted, and when I wanted. He did not say a word when I told him I was giving up my job to start my own project, Moiseum. He could have discouraged me. Many of my friends did not have support from their families when they were starting out with their projects. The families opposed it, even tried to forbid them to begin on such an uncertain path. My dad gave me freedom. And that was super important!

In Future...

I would like to have peace... But really... I cannot tell. I live from day to day. Just four years ago I was a student. I did not know what I would do in my life. So when you ask me what will it be in a few or several years, this is a cosmic perspective for me. I have two priorities—I would like to do what I want and have peace...

Different Take on Silicon Valley

Female Founders Program

In 2014, I went to Silicon Valley for a two-week long Female Founders program organized by Blackbox accelerator, with support from Google. Luckily the organizers financed my whole stay. This is because I think the *female founders only* idea was a mistake.

During our time at Blackbox we did not take part in outside events, we did not know how it was "in the real world" out there. We were strongly "incubated." It was the first edition, which included American women, before Blackbox accepted only foreign founders.

Blackbox offered interesting meetings. Yet the whole concept of a two-week mentoring program for 20 women, where there was no competition, nothing to win, where the participants are on the same level was completely surreal. As a teenager I attended a female school for six years so being around just women was nothing new to me.

It quickly turned out that most of the participants competed with each other in a secret, premeditated way, which I completely failed to fathom. Why? What for? For the first week I was shocked after seeing what was going on, not knowing why. The program was an interesting experience but I think that it would have worked better as a regular, mixed gender course. It would have had a greater potential and carried more value.

The Trap of *Females Only* Approach

At some point I felt extremely uncomfortable as a participant and group member. I began to wonder whether if it had been a mixed gender edition I would have even gotten into an acceleration program. For me, who created a start-up as a woman, participating in a program targeting just women was a waste of time, as it was an artificial selection. It had mostly a negative effect. I don't know what was the point. Was I supposed to get directed, was I supposed to not be afraid to continue working in start-up industry? It's hard to tell. I did not bring home anything like that.

The organizers created a trendy *Females Only* program and got involved in a fashionable subject. They can write this project into their annual report.

Seven Thousand App Store Reviews

When we did a summary at the end of the program it turned out that my simple DailyArt application was quite a strong offer compared to others. First, it had great traction and retention, did not need outside investors, and had 7,000 positive App Store reviews. And many users who were sending me several e-mails a day telling me the app was great and asking to keep going!

Different Way

I know the limits of DailyArt. It is a small application and I realize how much I can grow it. If I got into a real accelerator I am afraid I might fall into the trap of "digging myself into the sandbox" or I would need to show a steady few percent growth. I would need to get strong financing. But this is not what I want in my life. Maybe my goals are not overly ambitious but at the same time the culture of "pumping up" projects is not very appealing to me. I would like to come to Silicon Valley for vacations… Also, to prove that you can do things a different way, that you don't need to just focus on fighting for the next financing round…

On Cultural Differences and Inspirations in a Museum

It is only when I went on scholarship to California that I understood why 70 percent of DailyArt users were from the United States, why they were the ones who will want to download it and pay for it. Compared with the Europeans, and especially with Poles, the Americans have a totally different approach to art. Polish people greatly revere art, in an almost religious way. In Europe we have many old churches and temples. Art is strongly connected with religion. Maybe this is where the pious approach comes from.

The Europeans have a complex attitude toward art. In France talking about art is considered snobbish. When talking about art, people stress their education, their refinement. And yet, the general level of education in society is not very high, both in Poland and worldwide.

But in the United States, people visit a museum to listen to lectures during which they ask questions and receive answers. They participate in a discussion. They take part in a community. For the Americans talking about art does not need to be highbrow. Art is something worth knowing about, worth learning something new about because it is an integral element of our civilization, a part of our everyday life. The Americans see inspiration and beauty in art. In Poland no one says, "I'm going to a museum for inspiration." But in the States such culture exists. This is a cultural difference. To notice it and understand it you need to go and spend some time in the United States.

On Mentoring

Mentors in the Life of Start-ups

The role of mentors is very important but I discovered it only after joining an acceleration program in Silicon Valley. There the start-up community functions in a completely different level compared to Poland. In Silicon Valley you can find real mentors. At home, in Poland, we don't have them yet and those we have are not in the same league as those in the Valley. They cannot function in the same way, nor can they understand how to get along with young people.

The Polish start-up scene has not yet had big time successes. Those that are considered big in Poland happen daily in Silicon Valley and are considered average. It's just a different scale of success. And another time-space continuum. In Poland many things happen slowly. And before certain trends have reached us they are already established in Silicon Valley or already passé.

As a Mentor...

Sometimes I act as a mentor but my mentoring has nothing to do with the mentoring in Silicon Valley. I am trying to help the start-ups that lack experience. I talk to people during start-up weekends. I like to help people and try to point out on where they should focus. I tell them to advertise not just in Poland but to create their website in English to be visible on the global Internet. These are just basic things, details. Unfortunately people often get stuck in their old patterns.

I can talk to people who are very daunted, as I have worked out many things over the past years. I can tell them not to be afraid or to think before they act, or to follow up the initial impact and catch the bull by the horns. On the other hand I don't want this advice to sound too much like a command.

Thrown into Deep Water

The start-ups which left Poland and now are operating in Silicon Valley or were there for a while and now came back to our market represent a whole different class of a company—Estimote, Growbots, UXPin being some good examples of global firms with global successes. Piotr Wilam of Innovation Nest has the principle that people with interesting ideas need to be "catapulted" out of Poland and thrown into the deep water of Silicon Valley. Such an approach is just what Polish start-ups need but it is not yet widely practiced. The start-ups in which Piotr Wilam invests get a whole new perspective. Founders working with Piotr leave the Valley much wiser. You need to go to Silicon Valley and learn there.

Absorb Knowledge

One day Piotr Wilam asked me if I wanted to go to the States. I said yes, but I was more interested in New York which has many museums and is a large city. I asked what Silicon Valley really was and what was I supposed to do there. And I went to Silicon Valley. I still feel my stomach cramp at the thought of how stupid I was. Piotr Wilam always chuckles when he remembers what I said.

Today I am all set up to work remotely. I can be anywhere and keep working. I would like to come to the Valley more often, stay for a few weeks, maybe a few months to absorb more knowledge and draw from the innovation of the place. At the same time Silicon Valley is not a place where I would like to live. It is not my place.

Women in Start-up Industry

Question of Upbringing?

Women approach success differently than men. Women care about tangible things. And tangible things are sometimes difficult to sell. I know girls who are scared of talking about their successes. I don't really know why. I met many professionally active women doing lots of interesting things but I hear about their successes 80 minutes into the conversation...

I know some who are respected figures in the start-up community, who organize fantastic, valuable events. But they don't talk about their successes, they don't boast. Maybe it is a question of upbringing?

I Feared the Unknown

Why are there so few women in the start-up world? Maybe they are afraid. I remember myself wondering if I should go to the Startup Weekend. First, I was scared. Second, I was scared I knew no one. I was scared no one would like me. I was afraid of the unknown. These are terrible feelings, but common.

Maybe men don't have such fears. Maybe they don't wonder if people will like them...

Risk

Women are more responsible than men and are more afraid of risk. They don't want to involve people in projects that might not get off the ground, which don't yet have funding. My professional path is very safe. I work and make money as a result but I make the money myself. I would never offer my team to get each a five percent share or to create a company, and for now we work for free. I would never take such a risk.

Male World

I've never had a problem working with men. I've never had a problem with being blond with a *tweeting voice*. I don't know where lies the problem of male–female work relations. Although I know it exists.

If I don't know something I never hide it. I don't know how to code but I have trusted collaborators who do. I've never said I was the Alpha and the Omega. I've always stressed that my education is in art history and if someone has a problem with it, that's their business.

However, museums employ mostly women but directors' positions are usually reserved for men; women hold lower positions.

Advice for Women

I would like women to do their thing, not to be discouraged and not to give in to setbacks as these things happen to everyone. When girls want to create something, let them go for it. Let them build their companies and their start-ups.

Women's Organizations

… sometimes can stress dependence, I am afraid. I am not a member of any women's organizations and I usually don't participate in meetups for women. Yet if those organizations become springboards getting women ready to function in the real male–female world, if such a format can work it should be promoted. If something needs to be incubated, it should be done. Yet if meetings for women are organized only because of the fact that we are women and "women should support each other because it's a bad, bad world out there" such an approach is silly and leads nowhere. You should, however, present role models. You should invite wise girls who do interesting things and radiate positive energy. At the same time you should make sure that women's events produce results and don't lead to forming cliques, as this is not the effect we want.

You Can Have a Child and a Start-up

I know a couple who recently had a baby. Both mom and dad are start-uppers. So it can work. You can have a child and a start-up. Maybe some girls think that when they start a family, they will have to withdraw from professional life. Such thinking is the result of media propaganda where we keep hearing that having kids means the end of professional life for women and the world of mothers is restricted to the home. The media keep spinning the subject of difficulties in returning to work after maternity leave. Examples that show the reverse are seldom publicized.

In Poland It's a Bit Better

In Poland's start-up world there are many girls who like casual style and others who are very feminine. There is no culture of all-male start-ups in Poland. When I was in Silicon Valley many people told me stories of sexism in tech. Reportedly, it is common that wives forbid husbands—investors—to meet with female founders. Or that a start-up founded by a women will get funding only if a co-founder is a man. I cannot imagine such a situation in Poland. I cannot imagine talking to an investor and being refused financing because I am a woman! Maybe in some respects things are a bit better in Poland.

Final Note

We Are a Start-up from Poland

For me it is unthinkable that a Polish start-up does not identify with Poland. Most users of DailyArt know that we are a Polish start-up. Even if only because we make spelling mistakes in English captions to the paintings. No one makes an issue of the fact we are from Poland! Many users ask me about Poland, and write that their grandparents came from Poland.

When, during a project organized in cooperation with the Ministry of Culture and National Heritage, DailyArt showed pre-WWII buildings in Warsaw we got great positive feedback from thousands of international users. Poland's history is very tragic and so it was a serious historical project. I don't see any reason why someone would like to hide the fact that they are from Poland. I don't think the founders of Skype had a problem with being from Estonia.

I am a proud Pole and I know that a team of people with whom I work also support the DailyArt welcome message: *Greetings from Warsaw, Poland.*

***

The interview took place on June 24, 2015 in Warsaw and San Francisco.

CHAPTER 6

Geek Girls Carrots

When Girls Code

Kamila Sidor—entrepreneur, social activist, founder of Geek Girls Carrots global community. She wants more women to work in IT. Thanks to Geek Girls Carrots already over 2,000 women learned to code. Her many social campaigns attract girls to new technology. Today Geek Girls Carrots exists in 14 countries.

> *Life is not about me helping you, if you help me. But about you helping me, me helping someone else and that someone helping someone else still… According to the "pay it forward" rule in Silicon Valley.*
> **—Kamila Sidor**

I meet Kamila in San Francisco. This year she came to California to rest and to go to the annual Burning Man festival at Black Rock Desert in Nevada. Kamila regularly visits Silicon Valley to breathe some "Valley air of innovation" and get energized for her next challenge.

She tells me that it is worthwhile to chase your dreams, it is worth to believe in oneself and what's most important—it's good to support others.

Dreams Fulfilled

The First Computer

All the money from my First Communion gift I spent on a Commodore 64. It was a great experience. I wanted it to play games, of course!

My dad took me to the computer store to get it. I remember clearly how we couldn't wait to unpack those boxes! We started unpacking them right in the car.

You'll Be a "Marketer"

At home I was encouraged to study science; in high school I was in a math-science curriculum. My dad got offended when I did not go to Warsaw University of Technology, although I was accepted there. I chose geography instead; a year later, I applied again and was accepted into the marketing and business administration program at the Warsaw School of Economics. My dad did not understand why I did not want to study technology, since with a technology degree it is easier to find a good job. He laughed that I would be "a marker."[1]

Dream Come True?

I graduated from Warsaw School of Economics. As a student I dreamed about working for an international corporation and participating in international projects. My dream came true. Although I quickly learned that this type of work was not for me, I was very disappointed. I had dreamed a dream which did not fit my need for self-realization and growth.

I Met My People

At the same time I started getting together with a friend (Tomek Kolinko), who worked, and still does, in tech start-ups. He always took part in relevant events, although in those days there was really just one start-up event—Aula Polska (*Polish Aula*). I went to those meetings once a month and really liked the start-up community. I felt I had met my people, people who want to be creative, who believe that you can change the world. These people were active, open-minded and full of new ideas that they were consistently turning into reality. I liked that mentality a lot. That was the beginning of my start-up adventure. Earlier I had worked in various places: in a bank, in an employment center, in tourism.

First Startup Weekend

Eighty percent of success is showing up—this is one of Woody Allen's favorite quotes. I showed up in places where one could meet interesting people,

---

[1] In Polish it says: "marker" and it comes from word "marketing"; world "marker" doesn't exist in Polish, it is a word play in Polish. Her dad was saying: "You will be a marker."

where interesting things were happening. I followed closely what was going on in the start-up ecosystem.

During one of those meetings I met my future boss who at the time planned the first Startup Weekend in Poland. I got invited to help coordinate that event. My job was to organize it. I accepted the challenge. It was a great success!

Stepping Up My Career

English was the official language of the first Startup Weekend. We hosted many international mentors. Organizing and participating in this event helped me get noticed in Poland's start-up ecosystem. I developed my network. That first Startup Weekend gave me a great boost of energy and was a huge step forward in my career.

First Investment

My partner at the time was building his next start-up and I decided to invest in it. I got shares in the company. At the same time I kept attending many events; on a daily basis watching the process of start-up development at home. This was the beginning of my career in the start-up industry although I did not have tech education, I am not a techie and I cannot even code.

Girls

"Plus Ones"

Organizing Startup Weekend, I spent a lot of energy pitching the event to women—I wanted them to come, to speak and to actively participate. I turned for help to a friend, (Ola Sitarska), who had already done some start-up projects. Ola appeared in the media explaining why it was worthwhile to come to such events and encouraged girls to take part. We had a pool of discounted tickets meant especially for ladies.

I told my boss that my goal for the Startup Weekend was for half of the participants to be female. I did a whole range of marketing actions around this idea but ultimately I failed. Of 120 participants there were 10 women. It also turned out that half of the girls were "plus ones"—they came with their partners.

I decided to change that.

Girls

I thought that it would make sense to organize tech meetings for girls. With my programmer girlfriend we started planning a specific event that would have the word *girls* in the name. No one could then complain that the event was not for women. The first meeting took place in July 2011 in Warsaw. It had 11 participants, mainly our friends.

We Don't Complain

The girls liked our idea but already at the first meetup we heard complaints about how hard it was for women in IT. I did not want to create a "complainers' club" but instead a community with a positive message that would encourage girls to activity.

Wrocław

Initially building an organization for women was just a side gig. Still, soon my actions gained momentum. I began to devote more of my time and energy to building this community.

Our first Warsaw meetings were mentioned on antyweb.pl blog. As soon as the information appeared I was contacted by a girl from Wrocław (Kasia Marchocka), who asked me if she could organize a similar event. I wasn't sure, I replied, but suggested we should talk. This is how we created meetups in Wrocław.

Other Cities

Later we got contacts in other cities and when those centers were established girls from other places kept joining… It was amazing. I had never dreamed of such growth. We were already in 10 cities even though I still had no procedure on how to add new chapters to *Geek Girls Carrots*. At every point I was sure that it was "the last town that wanted to join us."

Berlin

Meanwhile my friend Kamila Stępniowska, who worked hand in hand with me establishing the organization, went to a conference in Berlin and there met another Polish woman who got very interested in our activity. When she got back from the conference she said: "Our next city is Berlin!"

Soon the girls from Berlin visited us in Warsaw and we started working together. We began to get offers from more cities all over the world. Initially we were contacted just by Poles who had gone abroad and wanted to get involved. Now we hear from girls from all over the world. We became a global organization.

Geek Girls Carrots

Flying Fish

There are two schools of marketing. One says that the company's name is essential, it defines the values of the organization and the product.

Another school teaches that the name is not important. What is crucial is the product, which must meet the expectations and needs of its users. And even if the product is called "Osram" (a light bulb brand name; also, a taboo word in Polish) people will buy it anyway.

In the case of Geek Girls Carrots I followed the latter school. In 2007, my friend and I were planning to open an alternative travel agency. We called it "Flying Fish." For six months we worked on the logo, the website color scheme, the slogan, and so on. But when everything was ready the project failed to take off because after all our marketing tasks we had never taken the time to find out if our business plan made any sense. We never even created a prototype. That setback taught me that the name isn't essential. What is important is to start operating. You have to get the product to the market and see whether someone wants to buy it.

Carrots or Pizza?

When we started our women's organization we did not spend much time on coming up with a name. We decided that *geek girls* sounded too generic. We decided to add another element. We asked ourselves what was associated with geek culture. Pizza! But pizza is unhealthy... And we wanted to create something different, something especially for the girls. We wanted something not associated with fast food and an unhealthy lifestyle. This is where the *carrots* came from. We decided on an English version. So we called ourselves Geek Girls Carrots. Somewhat by accident. It took us literally three minutes to come up with this name. After our bad experiences we did not want to wrack our brains on terminology... we just wanted to get to work.

The name turned out to be a good fit. Everyone asks about it. Carrots became our symbol. We have the color, the gadgets, carrot mascots, even carrot cookies. It is a distinctive symbol that we use to promote our work through the companies that cooperate with us. At many conferences our carrots are used as the background for photo ops. But no one would use our images if our brand was associated with something boring. What's essential is the quality of the product and the service.

No Institutional Backing

Four years ago I did not expect our organization to grow so fast. If I had to decide what I needed money for, I would have said, "I am establishing a programming community for 20 girls and organizing a meeting in Warsaw." That one sentence would have summed up our whole activity. Luckily I did not write our bylaws or business plan because created too early they could have limited our flexibility. From the very beginning we were a grassroots organization, not backed up by any corporation or institution.

When Facebook offered to organize a recruiting event for us we agreed and it soon came about that recruitment meetings became one of our sources of income. Since we did not have any business plan we were able to listen to the needs of the market. We've been open to various forms of cooperation; although now, after being on the market for four years, we know our value.

Nonprofit

The organization is registered in my name. We are a nonprofit. There are three principles of our operation: all the profits go to social causes and the running of Girl Geek Carrots. Some employees work full-time, others work with us pro bono and just develop their skills. We cooperate with companies who support our social mission, which is getting women interested in new technologies.

Good PR

Good PR is crucial to our organization—we make sure to get media coverage, we participate in many conferences. When we create a buzz, companies or potential event organizers find us easily and get in touch.

Geek Girls Carrots doesn't have a marketing department but we do rely on public relations and, Maja Sztenke is in charge of that. We make sure that the media invite our specialists and technology experts. We cooperate with the media to show as many female role models as possible. With our activity we want to reach young girls and women who would not come to our meetings but are looking for a path for themselves. Via press, radio, and TV, we can show them inspiring stories of women in IT.

How We Get Financing

We work with many firms. Companies recruit workers via our organization, using our Internet channels and commission us to organize meetings. Some enterprises buy our programming workshops, which are free for the participants and consequently get access to potential workers. These are very helpful initiatives because usually the workshop participants are women—it eases their career paths, opens up lots of possibilities. At every workshop we discover some gems—girls with fantastic programming talents who, although they might not yet know how to code, learn very fast. We always look for such people. Companies can look for employees for their teams through our ads and enhance their *branding* by becoming our partner. Our organization is respected by many parties. We don't just help girls. We are an integral part of the start-up ecosystem and IT industry.

My Salary Is Below Average

On Internet forums you can find many comments on us. Some people say we got money from the EU. This is not true. You can look into our finances which are maybe not the best but we are still going through the stage of intensive growth. You can read the financial report of the first three years of our operation—one can see where the money comes from, how much we have, and how we spend.

Important Conversation

I once met Jurek Owsiak.[2] We talked about Internet hate. Owsiak says that as I create larger, more important events I will encounter more hatred. He told me to always remember in such moments why I started this work, what were my core values. This is what make us what we are and it should be the bedrock of our activity. If I remember that advice, no one will be able to break me.

Our Meetings

It's Worthwhile to Catch Up

After two years of organizing regular meetups, we began also to hold programming workshops—Code Carrots, which are weekend quarterly programming workshops in Python, JS, SQL, and Java. These are popular courses taught by excellent programmers. We want to show girls that learning and growing pays off, giving them the opportunity to learn how to code and encouraging them to update their skills and competencies.

Meetups

Our meetups have a simple format: the official part, the lecture, then networking and socializing. Networking and chatting, often over a beer, are the two key elements of our events. We want to attract girls to our organization and teach them to mix with various people, grow their networks. Sometimes we organize games to get people off their seats and at the same time demonstrate how important it is to communicate and get to know each other. Without the ability to create business relations, maintaining them and using them won't get us anywhere in either a corporation or a start-up. At some point someone has to recommend us.

The leaders are encouraged to organize interesting meetups. Friendly atmosphere determines the quality of any event. Creative speakers

---

[2] Jerzy Owsiak: A founder and President of the Wielka Orkiestra Świątecznej Pomocy (WOŚP), one of the largest nongovernmental, nonprofit, charity organizations in Poland.

who share their experience are also the key to a successful meeting and featuring technology gadgets like Oculus, AirWheel, OneWheel, 3d printers, Sphero balls help develop fun atmosphere. There's a lot happening at Geek Girls Carrots events.

End of the World or an Easy Hurdle

The lecture is not the main part of a meeting; the important thing is that people turn up and get to know each other. When people meet, "magic" might happen. Direct interaction often means creating and implementing new ideas, which might open new possibilities.

We can meet someone facing problems similar to ours, which in turn will help us solve them. We will not feel alone with our insecurities. By talking to people, something that seemed like the end of the world turns out to be an easy hurdle.

Moments of Weakness

I could tell many stories of girls who tried to build their projects but lacked self-confidence, who say they are not entrepreneurs and don't have the knack for business. Only after coming to our meetup and listening to the presentation of a person who had successfully accomplished a project do they understand that moments of despair and self-doubt are completely normal! We all have moments of weakness and bad days. Entrepreneurs go through times of doubt. It is not that I cannot cope or don't have a talent for business. Our speakers often become mentors to young women who are starting up.

Presentations

We have presentations during which we get shown ultramodern solutions and concepts. The girls tell stories of how their interests and careers evolved, how they got from point A to B. "I studied humanities and now I'm a Java programmer." Such stories are motivating. A friend of mine, who after studying psychology learned coding at the Code Carrots, today works as a programmer—she teaches and writes workshop scripts.

I remember a lecture when our speaker demonstrated how to animate illustrations. During a 30-minute session she animated a drawing and proved to us that movie making applications were not so scary.

Without Men It Is Impossible to Change the World...

Men are also the organizers of our meetups, although they are in the minority. Gentlemen are welcome in Geek Girls Carrots and we are very grateful for their assistance and involvement. Without men it is impossible to change the world because social change needs wide social support. If men don't want to have more female colleagues in IT companies we will not force that change. Men must be open to changes, too.

The Team

The Team—Communications

At the moment our team has about 90 members, we are all a part of a closed group on Facebook. It is hard to say where our organization starts or ends—even I don't know all the people active under the Geek Girls Carrots umbrella. I am in touch only with the main organizers. We tried many communication tools and it turns out Facebook is the most effective—all of us Carrots have FB accounts so there is no need to build another system.

Every country is different and has its own proven customs or principles. For instance in the United States there is Meetup. That's why depending on where we operate we will use popular channels of local communication.

After Hours Project

For most people, Geek Girls Carrots is an additional after hours project. At the moment we have just full time employees and for the remaining organizers it is an after work diversion from everyday routine and a chance of acquiring new skills. Our organizers learn to manage people, projects, web content, social media promotion or script writing, there is always more room for learning.

At work we don't always have the chance to acquire new skills and competencies that are required for promotion or changing jobs.

Organizers who leave us, usually keep in touch while building their own careers. A good example is a friend of mine, who started out as my assistant (Katarzyna Frąszczak) after two years of hard work she became my deputy. Today she is leaving the project to develop her own career abroad. Geek Girls Carrots is a big step forward in our careers.

Help and Be Helped

People who join Geek Girls Carrots sometimes have no experience but would like to gain it, that's why for me an ideal candidate is a person who will say straight up she wants to learn! We address our social programs to people who want to get involved. I think it is essential that the participants in the social projects are open to both giving and receiving, taking advantage of an opportunity. Unfortunately women have tendency to help others rather than seek support.

Mentoring

In Geek Girls Carrots we stress the importance of mentoring and the exchange of knowledge. Our organizational structure is flat and the girls acting locally have no bosses. That's why new people can sometimes feel lost and don't know how to navigate the organization. We keep accumulating know-how and record our knowledge in the manual but what's most effective is mentoring. Every new organizer gets a helper with at least one-year experience. Our international experience is also very valuable. An example of an excellent mentor was Paulina Bagińska from Berlin who mentors Vanadana Gupta who is developing a new chapter of Carrots in New Delhi, India.

Globally

Up till now we've implemented our projects in 14 countries. We are in Japan, South Korea, Portugal, Ireland, and the Czech Republic, to name just a few.

Recently I spoke with girls from Tel Aviv. I met them through Monika Synoradzka, our former organizer from Poznań. In this way we operate and make contacts, find out about one another and begin to work together. Many women want to collaborate with us since we share the approach to the issue of females in IT: we want as many women in technology as possible but at the same time we don't exclude men. We use the language of positive communication and give women "fishing rods, not fish."

Freedom of Action

Geek Girls Carrots organizers enjoy independence in decision making. We also have a simple rule—if there is a problem the organizers contact me, in crisis situations I step in. I am always available and I can be convinced to make some changes, although sometimes I stick to my decisions. The girls independently build their teams and implement their rules. We do not have stiff regulations. The organizers themselves know best what their local communities need.

Leader

A good leader can present his or her mission to the team so the employees can identify with it. Team members should feel that the mission is not just their professional vision, but also their life vision. A good leader knows the strengths and the weaknesses of the team and creates a clear framework for the organization's structure so every member of the group can fulfill their professional ambitions and develop their competencies. Most people progress when they are given the space for action and the freedom to make decisions. When they are respected, they identify with their project and devote maximum time to it. Such employees will not just be involved in their job but also professionally fulfilled.

Of course some people demand clear, specific orders and are motivated by monitoring. In practice, however, such persons choose tasks that are less ambitious and as a result they make slower progress. It is up to the leader to find a place for them in their organization, if there is one.

After Action Review

Sometimes we all encounter failure. In such cases we don't look for a witch to burn at the stake but work together analyzing the situation and identify what went wrong. After completing all the projects, we do an after-action review. This is our favorite method to assess projects. We evaluate what went well, what makes us proud, what we can repeat, and what we can do better. We always write down the most important points of the meeting and update our manuals.

We give each other honest feedback about what didn't work and we make new decisions. I always ask why things happened the way they did and what we could have done better. At the same time we analyze our mistakes. In my opinion this works really well.

Effectiveness

People who take part in social projects or start-ups are motivated by the wish to learn and develop. Start-ups can teach you what corporations won't. Start-ups are about rapid development, changes, making money. Social projects are about sharing. The common denominator is flexibility combined with effectiveness, which often lacks in large companies.

Together We Create a Wider Coalition

Geek Girls Carrots was the first project in Poland addressed to women in tech and IT. It was annoying when new, analogous groups started sprouting. I asked a rhetorical question: why do they start a new community while we are already there? But a friend of mine convinced me that it's worthwhile to learn from one another. I observed what other groups were doing better and in my next projects I did not repeat their mistakes. Watching your competition helps identifying the solutions that work without testing them yourself. I realized we were all a part of a wider coalition and accepted that while some people are attracted to Geek Girls Carrots, others prefer different groups. At present we cooperate with competing groups and even hold joint meetings.

Recently we had 581 candidates for our programming workshops, for only 40 available spots. We are unable to meet all the demand.

With start-ups it is similar, new business models are being tested on a regular basis. Competition means more people are active in the same field, they introduce new solutions. This is of great value. You just need to know how to use it.

On Important Moments

I Feel Moved

Today it seems almost unbelievable that my organization, which I created from scratch with one friend, is present in 27, soon 30 cities! The size of the organization and its international character is overwhelming and requires great responsibility. Thanks to our efforts, 2,000 people have learned how to code! When I look back on our history I am very moved. When I receive birthday greetings from people I don't know and who tell me how my organization changed their lives, it feels great.

I believe my projects are important and needed and will influence people's lives. Finally, the fact that I don't work for a corporation or for someone else, but instead realize my own ideas, makes me happy.

Successes Small and Large

In the past few years, we have continued to expand our organization overseas. For me it's a giant success. Recently I got pictures from various places, among them from Tokyo—the photo shows a group of 50 Japanese women with our symbol. These moments are precious.

There are other uplifting events. Not long ago I was invited to a meeting at the Presidential Palace, not as a tourist but a conference participant. I was the only woman among the speakers and the only one under fifty. I was speaking on behalf of young entrepreneurs.

I was also invited to a cup of tea with the Duchess of Luxembourg, we discussed the problems of educational systems.

Every time I receive such an invitation I feel honored. It is important that our voices are being heard. We keep having small successes. For me they are like points on a map, which at the end of my life will form a beautiful picture.

On Future

Future

I would like to do other social projects. At some point I will probably decide to give up my "Carrots." That will happen when I create a structure solid enough for the organization to run by itself. To be able to leave with no worries I have to address many weaknesses of the organization which are connected to my own personality and character. I have noticed that wherever I encounter problems, so does my organization. If I cannot, or don't want to do something all the shortcomings show up in Geek Girls Carrots. I have new ideas for other social and educational projects, which I would like to implement...

All Over the World...

Our organization has been expanding rapidly. We have a plan to grow tenfold. I think this is feasible. We want to organize more meetings and have our blueprints and programming scripts used all over the world. Our goals are very ambitious. We have our aspirations to expand, which means we want to organize more regular events. My team, working full time, is overwhelmed. This slows things down. I am also a factor in the slow-down. So soon we need to prepare a strategy of development, which will be another milestone.

Women in IT

Stand on Your Own Two Feet

I have my own theory why there is a gap between men and women working professionally. Men are raised to fight, compete, conquer, prove their worth and masculinity to the world. Society rewards them for sharing their knowledge and being active in the business sphere. Women are not taught those skills in their socio-educational path or while growing up. Girls are taught to sit tight and wait until they are called and praised— then we can feel singled out and satisfied. This makes it hard for us to step forward with our proposals, to self-promote. Sure it can be risky but we should not give up.

When a Woman Is Successful…

…her success is much talked about, there is more media coverage. Men who achieve similar successes are less talked about, as there is nothing interesting or unusual about it. This is why we encourage women to promote their own achievements. A successful woman impresses both women and men. She becomes a strong inspiration for both sides.

My Observation

There are all kinds of women in IT. This is beautiful, as thanks to our diversity we have a lot to offer to the world of technology. To be really simplistic, there are two types of women in IT—(probably more, but this is my personal observation). The first type are girls who believe themselves to be superwomen. They know the IT world very well, are popular and recognizable. They stand out. I was one of those women. I took part in many events, so everybody knew me. During events the male–female ratio is usually unequal, even as low as one to fifty. Some girls can take advantage of such situations. They run a company, employ programmers and are, for the most part, professionally fulfilled.

But there are also many people who are low key, who like to hide in the shadows. Women in IT, being a minority, are constantly subject to public scrutiny and criticism. IT girls are always in the limelight. For a sensitive, introverted person such a situation can be uncomfortable—they would likely withdraw and this is not easy. Minorities live in constant stress, become weary of being exposed. If in a team of five men there is one woman she will probably attract more attention, her mistakes will be immediately noticed and commented on. Being in an exposed place can be very stressful.

Qualifications

Another question connected to the presence of women in IT is the fact that society always questions our qualifications. I know a woman who fixes computers, working with hardware. Her clients always question her abilities and ask whether she would be able to do the repair. Every time she has to explain that it is her everyday job. She tried to be aggressive, and to stay calm. People don't trust her and ask her to consult with a male colleague. This is alarming in our society. People do not believe a woman can be competent doing "men's work."

Our society undermines women's feeling of self-worth. This is a cause for concern and should be changed.

Education of Women

There are too few women working in IT. We are raised to be good mothers, wives, housekeepers. Society charges us with responsibility for a peaceful home, creating a good atmosphere for the family. Women are not expected to be successful in business, making big money. In our culture a woman can stay at home or work professionally. Society accepts both roles. A man does not really have this choice. Although it has been changing in recent years.

Why are there not many women in IT? The answer is simple. Societies do not put much emphasis on the education of women. As a result girls do not have some skills that are essential in business.

Can You Be a Mom and a Career Woman?

Of course you can. Some women prove that you can do anything! The question is if we can divide our attention. We do not have to do everything ourselves. We just need to know what makes us fulfilled. An unhappy mom is not a cool mom. We should understand what we want for ourselves and what are the expectations of the society or our family. These matters should be separated. We have to honestly answer this question: who did I want to be when I was a little girl? It is worth revisiting.

Many women are successful in science while raising children and attending to their family. My personal idol is Professor Agnieszka Zalewska, chair of the CERN Council. She is the first woman in CERN elevated to such a high position. She is a professor of physics and a mother of five. It is possible to reconcile a professional career with kids and family? Yes, but not every one of us wants to choose this path.

You Can Manage!

In Warsaw the start-up women don't need to become more masculine. I think it is sometimes easier to be a girl in predominantly male environment. In Poland I've never heard stories such as those from Silicon Valley, when an investor after a business meeting invites a girl to dinner…

Start-up girls are much admired and perceived as go-getters although, unfortunately, there are still too few of us. My impression is that women too often choose the "warm slippers" as society rewards them for such behavior. They are not motivated, cheered to go forward. Women need support, someone who would just say: You can manage!

Three Pieces of Advice

Advice for Everyone—Be the Dumbest Person in the Room

My first piece of advice for everyone is to realize whose hand we are holding. Is our closest person supporting us? Will they support us when times become hard? Or maybe they will be complaining and blaming us for everything. Surrounding ourselves with valuable, supportive people is very important. When you come across someone who constantly criticizes your actions, you will probably not get very far. Very little can be achieved individually. We build our success cooperating with people. If it wasn't for my partner Tomasz it would have taken me much longer to get where I am now. When I was feeling discouraged, when I was coming home in low spirits, he would say: *It's only a moment of doubt, you do wonderful things, get to work and keep going!* Those words helped a lot and I am very grateful for to him for them.

Today I surround myself with friends who can "blow in my wings" but who also can be honest with me. I know they have good intentions and they want to support me in my activity. Sometimes I hear: *You will do it! Don't worry!* And sometimes they say honestly: *It must be your ego speaking!*

I have always had a simple strategy in my life—to be the dumbest person in the room. In my dorm I was the worst student of all my roommates. I always wanted to push myself up, to catch up to the best. I like to surround myself with people who believe in me, who are smarter than me and are three steps ahead of me, because they are the greatest inspiration.

Another Piece of Advice—Effectiveness, Keep Active!

The second matter concerns effective action and persistence. When we have something to do we just need to sit down and do it. If we don't know something we need to research. You should use what is already there. Don't spend weeks browsing the Internet, do something! The final goal should include the first step that I need to take to get going. This is my approach to work. It is worth testing.

Sometimes before making a decision I get stopped by fears—I try to accept them. And although I'm still scared I make the decision and act. It's like jumping with a parachute: you are afraid but you know you will survive. You just need to check the equipment. And then you are flying! You are living your life to the fullest! Boom!

Advice no. 3—Learn!

The third piece of advice might sound banal: we learn all our lives. Learning never stops. When someone says they are 30 and it's too late to learn programming I answer, *no, no, it's not too late!* It's never too late. We had a participant named Renata. She was about to retire and at 60 she started to learn programming. She wanted to create a website and have her own online store. She wanted to write the program herself. And she did it!

It doesn't matter how old you are. You have to move forward! And the fact is, we make mistakes. We fall, get back up. All this enriches our human experience. Today your company can be wonderful but in five years it might be worthless, because the technology will change. No need to wait for some special moment, you need to act now, because the moment is now.

On ideals

Role Models

It is important to have role models. I am very fond of what Ela Madej says and does. Her experience in business and at the same time her approachability and authenticity attract many people. She is effective in her work and at the same time maintains a healthy balance in her life.

I have also been watching Sheryl Sandberg. She started *Lean in* project about the same time I was starting mine. Of course the scale of these projects is completely different. After reading her book *Lean in: Women, Work and the Way to Lead* I realized that what we have in Poland is not so bad!

I like the biography of Marie Skłodowska-Curie and the story of her daughter. Sometimes I look at photos of physicists' reunions from the early 1900s. Maria Curie was the only woman but she looks at ease. Yet, she did break into the male dominated world of science.

"Women to the Tractors!"

Historically women in Poland managed large estates, especially when men during wars or revolutions died or were exiled to forced labor. Compared to the rest of the world Polish women got voting rights quite early, in 1918, while in Switzerland as late as in 1971. When men fought in WWII women worked in factories and during the Polish People's Republic (PRL) one of the slogans said "Women to the tractors!"—and they indeed began to drive tractors.

Family Inspirations

In my family I also have strong women. My great-grandmother as a young person immigrated to the United States. It was in 1897. She left from Poland Galicia region, she never returned there. In America she lived in Brooklyn where she started a business. Poland and America were worlds apart. There was terrible poverty in Poland. Still, my great-grandmother decided to come back to her country. She sold all her estate, took the money and a gun. She boarded a ship, where she gave birth to her second child. She came to Gdynia (a port city in Poland) to be with the family of her husband. Later, she took the kid, the gun, and the money and left for eastern Poland, where she spent the rest of her life. Her strength, determination, and courage inspire me to this day.

She lived almost to a hundred. I was six years old when she died. If you grow up with such role models, it does not even occur to you that there is something women can't do!

It Is Important to Support Others

In 2002, before going to college I went to Warsaw to attend a preparatory course for the entrance exams. For a month I stayed with auntie Helena. She fixed me breakfast, gave pocket money, and took good care of me. The woman I'd never met before took me under her wings. One day I asked her: *Auntie, how do I pay you back?* She answered: *Child, you don't need to pay me back, just help out someone else in your life.*

I often remember those words and compare it to *pay it forward* rule in Silicon Valley. If you help me, I will help someone else and they will help still someone else.

Girls You Have Helped

"It is important to believe in yourself. It's important to look at the person holding your hand…" This is my life philosophy. Girls thank me for talking them into programming. They thank me for finding a mentor.

I get messages in which girls tell me how Girls Geek Carrots matter in their life. They write they cannot make the meeting because they live in a small town but thanks to us they feel really motivated. They study by themselves, read our articles. Sometimes someone approaches me in the street and thanks me for the workshops or self-study guides available on the Internet.

Sometimes I regret not collecting those stories. I look forward. I never look back.

Link to the Future

I cooperate with many young people and participate in the program "Link to the Future" where I met with youth from small towns. With some of them we keep in touch for a long time, we discuss what studies to pursue, or whether it is worth traveling abroad, they rely on my advice and mentoring, because instead of learning from your own mistakes you can learn from mistakes of others. It is worth remembering.

Public Speakers' Club

I am a co-founder of *Speaking Elephants TM*—a public speakers' club. It was my first social project. I was very involved in my work. It is there that I realized that I find fulfillment in social projects. On my team I had people who today run many projects and companies. When we were joined by a newbie they always said: *Kamila, go talk to them, you are good at it.*

One story is still vivid in my mind. It was in the middle of summer, in July. I was very tired but after work went to a meeting to the club.

I was returning home after midnight. I entered the elevator, which had a large mirror. I looked at myself. I was completely exhausted; my head was killing me. I thought: *I have a headache, feeling sick, but I am happy, I am satisfied! This is the life I want! I want to have a job that would make me happy, even if I am to get home after midnight, totally wasted!*

Inhale, Exhale

Being an entrepreneur is like riding a roller coaster. One day you accept an achievement award, the next day you are facing bankruptcy. The fear that I might not cope, make the wrong decision or that my key workers abandon the project is with me every day. It will never leave me.

I am learning how to distinguish fear from instinct and common sense. Observing your emotions, thoughts, and feelings is very useful in this process. By building new habits and rituals I arm myself for the times of crisis. They will be my fallback and a starting point for new actions.

I get up at seven. Yoga. Coffee. Breakfast.

Evening—twenty minutes of meditation and a few pages of a book.

A few times a week I write in my diary the most important thoughts and events of the past few days. In difficult moments I start counting my breaths: inhale, exhale.

***

The interview was conducted on August 27, 2015 in San Francisco.

About the Author

Marta Zucker, Independent entrepreneur, Mentor, Published Author, Blogger. Marta's two recent books on the global success of Polish start-ups were published by PWN (the leading Polish provider of professional literature). Each book is a selection of six interview-driven stories told by the start-ups' founders. The second book is focused on female founders. Both publications have been very well-received in the start-up, business, academic, and women's communities. "Igrzyska talentów w Dolinie Krzemowej. Rozmowy z mistrzami start-upów." Warszawa, 2015 (*Talent Olympics in Silicon Valley: Conversations with startup masters.*)

"Kobiety globalne w świecie start-upów. Rozmowy w Dolinie Krzemowej." Warszawa, 2016 (*Global Women in the Start-up World: Conversations in Silicon Valley.*)

For the last three years Marta has been working with the start-up communities in Silicon Valley and Poland. She helps start-ups reach global markets for people, ideas, and capital and has authored numerous analysis reports, recently focusing on new technologies and Silicon Valley. Marta has worked for many years with Polish business consulting firm KarStanS Ltd.; she also consulted independently in New York. She can be reached at: https://linkedin.com/in/martazucker/

Index

OTHER TITLES IN THE ENTREPRENEURSHIP AND SMALL BUSINESS MANAGEMENT COLLECTION

Scott Shane, Case Western University, Editor

- *Open Innovation Essentials for Small and Medium Enterprises: A Guide to Help Entrepreneurs in Adopting the Open Innovation Paradigm in Their Business* by Luca Escoffier, Adriano La Vopa, Phyllis Speser, and Daniel Satinsky
- *The Technological Entrepreneur's Playbook* by Ian Chaston
- *Licensing Myths & Mastery: Why Most Ideas Don't Work and What to Do About It* by William S. Seidel
- *Arts and Entrepreneurship* by J. Mark Munoz and Julie Shields
- *The Human Being's Guide to Business Growth: A Simple Process for Unleashing the Power of Your People for Growth* by Gregory Scott Chambers
- *Understanding the Family Business: Exploring the Differences Between Family and Nonfamily Businesses, Second Edition* by Keanon J. Alderson

Announcing the Business Expert Press Digital Library

Concise e-books business students need for classroom and research

This book can also be purchased in an e-book collection by your library as

- a one-time purchase,
- that is owned forever,
- allows for simultaneous readers,
- has no restrictions on printing, and
- can be downloaded as PDFs from within the library community.

Our digital library collections are a great solution to beat the rising cost of textbooks. E-books can be loaded into their course management systems or onto students' e-book readers.
The **Business Expert Press** digital libraries are very affordable, with no obligation to buy in future years. For more information, please visit **www.businessexpertpress.com/librarians**. To set up a trial in the United States, please email **sales@businessexpertpress.com**.

www.ingramcontent.com/pod-product-compliance
Lightning Source LLC
Chambersburg PA
CBHW050102210326
41519CB00015BA/3797

9 781947 441699